at home with

magnolia

at home with

magnolia

Classic American Recipes from

the Owner of Magnolia Bakery

Allysa Torey

Photography by John Kernick

WILEY

John Wiley & Sons, Inc.

Copyright © 2006 by Allysa Torey. All rights reserved.

Photographs © 2006 by John Kernick.

Published by John Wiley & Sons, Inc., Hoboken, New Jersey.
Published simultaneously in Canada.

Designed by Cassandra J. Pappas

For general information about our other products and services, please contact our Customer Care Department within the United States at (800) 762-2974, outside the United States at (317) 572-3993 or fax (317) 572-4002.

Wiley also publishes its books in a variety of electronic formats. Some content that appears in print may not be available in electronic books. For more information about Wiley products, visit our web site at www.wiley.com.

Library of Congress Cataloging-in-Publication Data

Torey, Allysa.
    At home with magnolia : classic american recipes from the owner of Magnolia Bakery / Allysa Torey.
        p. cm.
    Includes index.
    ISBN-13: 978-0-471-75137-3 (cloth)
    ISBN-10: 0-471-75137-5 (cloth)
    1. Cookery, American.   2. Desserts.   I. Title.
    TX715.T687 2006
    641.5973--dc22

                                                                            2005029357

Printed in the United States of America

10   9   8   7   6   5   4   3   2   1

For my mother and father,

who showed me that I could do anything I wanted to do

contents

acknowledgments

Many, many thanks . . .

To my agent, Carla Glasser,

for believing in this book from the beginning,

and for putting up with all of my craziness

To my editor, Justin Schwartz,

and Wiley Publishing,

for thinking this book was a great idea,

and making it a reality

To Margaret Hathaway,

who worked with me on everything from testing recipes

to cultivating the gardens

and taking care of the dogs during the photo shoots,

and who makes it all really fun

To Tadhg,

for his endless amounts of support and love

And to my wonderful and extremely hardworking staff at Magnolia,

who make it possible for me to spend most of my time in the country,

doing what I love to do.

introduction

This book is a long time in the making. After writing two bakery cookbooks, I'm thrilled to finally put together a collection that includes not only desserts but all of my favorite recipes that I've been making at home for friends and dinner guests for years.

Most of my life is spent cooking, baking, gardening, talking about food, and writing about food. I'm very lucky to live with someone who is as enthusiastic about eating as I am. When we have houseguests visiting for the weekend, they think it's a bit crazy when over our first cup of coffee we've already planned out our menu for the entire day. I love food. I love creating new recipes. I love when I open up the fridge to see a wide array of beautiful fresh ingredients and can spend a lazy afternoon puttering around the kitchen, preparing a meal just for the two of us, or a simple dinner on the back porch for neighbors on a summer evening.

I like to cook simple foods made with seasonal ingredients. I'm just about as passionate about gardening as I am about food. I have a cottage garden filled with roses and old-fashioned flowers and a large organic kitchen garden where I grow most of the vegeta-

bles we eat. The greatest thing about having your own garden is being able to run out barefoot and pick a few ears of corn or a handful of green beans. You can't get any fresher than food grown in your own backyard, and it really is amazing what a difference such fresh ingredients have in the outcome of your dishes.

What I don't grow myself, I get at the farmers' market, which is a wonderful option for high quality, locally grown and raised foods. It's very important for me to know where my food comes from. Living in the country gives me the opportunity to get to know and support the farmers who are raising the animals and growing the fruits and vegetables that end up on our kitchen table. My local farmers' market is also a great place for fresh dairy and eggs, artisanal cheeses, and a wide variety of organic meats.

I know that many people go to the grocery store and are able to buy any foods they want all year round, but I choose to cook primarily with seasonal produce. I find it satisfying to eat foods only when they're at their peak, and when they're out of season, rather than feeling deprived because I'm not eating them, for me there's the sweet anticipation of enjoying them the next year. I appreciate that there are only a few weeks in the summertime when I can bring home the perfect juicy nectarines or gorgeous ripe strawberries to make a pie, and that there are bushels of tomatoes for summer salads and pasta sauces for only a couple of months. In the winter, when there are piles of snow outside, there's nothing more comforting than staying inside the house in a cozy warm kitchen with a big pot of soup on the stove and a simple chocolate cake in the oven.

Although I love to spend time in the kitchen, I always try to keep things simple, and I avoid recipes that are fancy with unnecessary steps. A lot of people think they don't have the time, or they don't realize how quickly they can prepare a fresh, home-cooked meal. I like to spend some time early in the day preparing so that I can cook quickly, but in a relaxed manner in the evening. Especially when I'm entertaining, I find that if I prepare things in advance, I can really enjoy the time I have with my guests, whether it's a few friends from town, or the whole family up for a barbecue. It's less stressful for me, and so it's more fun for everyone.

I chop garlic, blanch vegetables, toast nuts, grate cheeses, prepare salad dressing, and just generally organize my ingredients and set them aside for later. I have friends with all kinds of different work schedules who make time in the morning to prepare, and find it makes it a lot easier to put together a healthy meal when they get home. Some of my friends with small children like to do this type of preparation for the next day's meals once the kids are put to bed.

By offering realistic options for everyday meals, I hope to encourage the home cook to make dinner any night of the week and get people back into the evening ritual of sitting down together around the table. I'd like to give people a well-rounded collection of simple recipes for all occasions.

I've organized the book into sections for starters, soups, lunches, dinners, sides, vegetables, and, of course, desserts. The dinners have been separated into two categories, weekday and weekend meals, which are based on how complicated the recipe is, and how long its preparation might take. These categories are just guides, though, and quick dishes with a nice presentation could easily be made when entertaining guests.

The recipes I've gathered here reflect the all-American sensibilities of my bakery and my home. My style is the same whether I'm making something sweet or savory—simple steps, fresh ingredients, and classic combinations.

at home with

magnolia

starters
appetizers and salads

corn fritters with chile-lime mayonnaise

makes 6 servings
(1 dozen fritters)

When I entertain I like to make something a little different that my friends wouldn't necessarily make for themselves at home. Corn fritters are a great appetizer to serve in the late summer when fresh corn is at its best, but frozen corn works just fine in this recipe as well.

¾ cup all-purpose flour

¾ cup yellow cornmeal

⅓ cup finely grated Locatelli Romano cheese

1 ½ teaspoon baking powder

¾ teaspoon salt

¼ teaspoon chili powder

1 ½ cups buttermilk

1 large egg, at room temperature

1 large egg yolk, at room temperature

1 ½ cups fresh or frozen corn kernels, blanched (see Note)

¾ cup chopped scallions (green parts only)

¼ cup olive oil

2 tablespoons unsalted butter

1 recipe Chile-Lime Mayonnaise (recipe follows)

About 1 ½ cups fresh or frozen corn kernels, blanched (see Note), for garnish

Lime wedges, for garnish

In a medium-size bowl, combine the flour, cornmeal, Romano cheese, baking powder, salt, and chili powder.

In a small bowl, beat the buttermilk with the whole egg and egg yolk and add to the dry ingredients, mixing until well combined. Stir in the 1 ½ cups corn and scallions.

Heat 2 tablespoons of the oil and 1 tablespoon of the butter in a large skillet over medium-high heat. Working in batches, spoon the batter (about 3 tablespoons for each fritter—an ice cream scoop works great for making these) into the skillet to make 3-inch fritters. Cook until golden, 3 to 4 minutes on each side, adding additional oil and butter as needed for each batch. Serve warm with the Chile-Lime Mayonnaise, garnishing with the additional 1 ½ cups corn kernels and lime wedges.

Note: To blanch fresh or frozen corn, bring a medium-size saucepan of cold water to a boil. Add the corn and cook until crisp-tender, 2 to 3 minutes. Remove from the heat, drain, and rinse under cold water.

chile-lime mayonnaise

makes about 1½ cups

1½ cups mayonnaise

2 tablespoons fresh lime juice

1 tablespoon minced jalapeño chile pepper (seeds and ribs removed)

2 teaspoons grated lime zest

This recipe comes from my friend Dave Cole, who owns Dave's Big Eddy Diner, our favorite restaurant near my home in Upstate New York. It can be served with the Crab and Crayfish Cakes (page 12) as well as the Corn Fritters.

Place all the ingredients in a small bowl and stir together until well blended.

eggplant with red and yellow cherry tomato sauce

makes 6 to 8 servings

This is my light and summery version of eggplant parmagiana. You can really taste the eggplant and the tomatoes since the sauce is cooked for a very short time and the eggplant goes in the oven for only a few minutes to just barely melt the cheeses.

eggplant

1 pound eggplant, peeled and cut into 1/3-inch-thick rounds

Salt

1 cup seasoned breadcrumbs

2 large eggs

1 cup olive oil

topping

1/2 recipe (about 1 1/2 cups) Red and Yellow Cherry Tomato Sauce (recipe follows)

1/2 cup ricotta cheese

1/2 pound fresh mozzarella, cut into thin slices (about 2 inches in diameter)

1/2 cup finely grated Locatelli Romano cheese

Preheat the oven to 350°F.

To make the eggplant: Place the eggplant slices on a wire cooling rack placed on a baking sheet, and generously salt on both sides. Let stand for 20 minutes, then pat dry thoroughly with paper towels. Place the breadcrumbs in a shallow bowl. Beat the eggs in a second shallow bowl. Working with one slice at a time, dip the eggplant in the egg and then dredge in the bread-crumbs until heavily and evenly coated. Transfer the eggplant to a baking sheet lined with waxed paper, arranging the slices in one layer only.

Heat 1/2 cup of the oil in a large skillet over medium-high heat. Add half of the eggplant, frying until crispy and golden brown, 5 to 7 minutes on each side. Transfer to a second baking sheet lined with paper towels. Add 1/4 to 1/2 cup more oil to fry the second half of the eggplant (the oil should be about 1/4 inch high in the skillet). (If the oil starts to burn, pour it out, wipe out the pan, and start with fresh oil.)

Transfer the second batch of eggplant to drain on the paper towels. Let cool for 1 to 2 minutes, then remove the paper towels. Put the baking sheet with the eggplant in the oven to keep warm.

Meanwhile, make the Red and Yellow Cherry Tomato Sauce.

Remove the eggplant from the oven and on each eggplant slice, layer 1 heaping tablespoon of the sauce, then 1 teaspoon of the ricotta, and 1 slice of the mozzarella. Lightly sprinkle the Romano cheese over the top.

Put the eggplant back in the oven for 3 to 4 minutes, until the cheese just begins to melt. Serve immediately.

red and yellow cherry tomato sauce

makes 3½ cups, enough for
1 pound of pasta

1 cup olive oil

4 tablespoons (½ stick) unsalted butter

1 cup finely chopped Vidalia onion

¼ cup minced garlic

4 cups halved mixed red and yellow cherry tomatoes, seeded

1 teaspoon salt

½ teaspoon freshly ground black pepper

½ cup chopped fresh basil

Cherry tomatoes are the first to ripen every summer in the garden, and you wind up picking a big basket every couple of days, it seems. I started making this sauce a few years back to use them all up.

Heat the oil and butter in a shallow Dutch oven over medium-high heat. Add the onion and garlic, reduce the heat to medium-low, and cook, stirring occasionally, until the onion is very tender, 8 to 10 minutes. Add the tomatoes, salt, and pepper, raise the heat to high, and stir occasionally until just tender, about 3 minutes. Remove from the heat and stir in the basil.

field greens with golden apples, goat cheese, and pecans

makes 6 servings

I've been making this salad for a long time. The raspberry vinaigrette is light and fruity with just a bit of cream, and it complements all of the ingredients in the salad very nicely. The recipe makes twice as much dressing as you need, but the rest can be stored in the refrigerator for up to a week and used at another time.

vinaigrette

¼ cup olive oil

¼ cup pineapple juice

¼ cup heavy cream

3 tablespoons red wine vinegar

3 tablespoons apple cider
(or apple juice)

1 tablespoon raspberry jam

Salt

Freshly ground black pepper

salad

12 cups mixed baby greens

1 ½ cups coarsely chopped
Golden Delicious apples
(about 2 medium)

1 ½ cups coarsely chopped
toasted pecans (see Note)

6 ounces soft fresh goat cheese,
crumbled

To make the vinaigrette: Place all of the ingredients in a blender or food processor and process until well blended.

To make the salad: Combine the greens with the apples, pecans, and goat cheese in a large bowl. Add about ½ cup of the dressing and toss to coat.

Note: To toast the pecans, place on a baking sheet in a 350°F oven for 15 minutes, or until lightly browned and fragrant.

risotto and mozzarella balls

makes 6 to 8 servings
(about 2 dozen)

I absolutely love risotto balls. I've never found anyone who doesn't love them. Sometimes I serve them over warm green beans tossed with a little olive oil and garlic and basil, but usually we just stand around the stove and eat them pretty much right out of the pan.

2 ½ cups cold Risotto (page 37)

1 cup plain breadcrumbs (use store bought—not fresh)

½ cup finely grated Locatelli Romano cheese

2 large eggs, beaten

⅓ pound fresh mozzarella, cut into ½-inch cubes

1 cup olive oil

Place the risotto, ½ cup of the breadcrumbs, Romano cheese, and eggs in a large bowl and blend with your hands until well combined. Using your hands, form the rice mixture into balls about 1½ inches in diameter. Poke a hole into the center of each ball, fill with a cube of the mozzarella, and close the hole over again with the rice mixture to enclose the cheese completely. Place the remaining ½ cup of breadcrumbs in a shallow bowl. Working with one ball at a time, roll the balls in the breadcrumbs until heavily and evenly coated. Transfer the rice balls to a baking sheet lined with waxed paper, arranging the balls in one layer only.

Heat ½ cup of the oil in a large skillet over medium-high heat. Add half of the rice balls, frying until crispy and golden brown all over, about 5 minutes. Transfer to a second baking sheet lined with paper towels, and tent with foil to keep warm. Add ¼ to ½ cup more oil to fry the second half of the rice balls (the oil should be about ¼ inch high in the skillet). Transfer the second batch of rice balls to drain on the paper towels, for 1 to 2 minutes. Serve hot.

yellow beet, walnut, and gorgonzola salad

makes 6 servings

The sherry shallot vinaigrette for this salad is very easy to make but is very flavorful. Sometimes I make it with tarragon vinegar instead of sherry vinegar, and sometimes I like to put corn in the salad as well—it's great with the beets and the blue cheese.

beets

6 medium-size yellow beets, stems and roots removed

3 tablespoons olive oil

Coarse salt

vinaigrette

1/4 cup sherry wine vinegar

2 tablespoons minced shallot

1 tablespoon Dijon mustard

3/4 cup olive oil

salad

12 cups mixed baby greens

3/4 cup coarsely chopped toasted walnuts (see Note)

1/2 cup crumbled Gorgonzola cheese (about 2 1/2 ounces)

Preheat the oven to 400°F.

To roast the beets: Cut the beets in half and place in a foil-lined baking pan. Toss with the 3 tablespoons of olive oil and season with the coarse salt. Seal the baking pan with a second piece of foil and roast until the beets are tender when pierced with a fork, about 1 hour. Let cool slightly, then remove the skins, and cut into slices about 1/4 inch thick. Set aside.

To make the vinaigrette: In a small bowl, whisk together the vinegar, shallots, and mustard. Slowly whisk in the 3/4 cup oil until well blended.

To make the salad: Combine the greens with the beets, walnuts, and Gorgonzola in a large bowl. Add the dressing and toss to coat. Serve immediately.

Note: To toast the walnuts, place on a baking sheet in a 350°F oven for 10 minutes, or until lightly browned and fragrant.

pumpkin ravioli with corn, hazelnuts, and asiago

makes 6 to 8 servings

This is a very traditional Italian pasta dish, which I've changed up a bit and added a couple of things. It's wonderful as a starter for an autumn dinner when you're serving something simple like roast chicken for your main course. I also make this quite often for lunch, since it's so easy to put together . . . and so delicious.

1 pound fresh or frozen pumpkin ravioli (or butternut squash ravioli)

1/2 cup (1 stick) unsalted butter

1/4 cup minced shallots

1 cup fresh or frozen corn kernels, blanched (see Note)

1/2 cup coarsely chopped toasted hazelnuts (see Note)

1/2 teaspoon salt

3 tablespoons coarsely chopped fresh sage

1/2 cup freshly grated Asiago cheese

Put a large pot of water on to boil over high heat. Cook the ravioli according to the package directions; the time will vary depending upon whether you're using fresh or frozen ravioli. Drain the ravioli and set aside.

Melt the butter in a large skillet over medium-high heat. Add the shallots, reduce the heat to medium, and cook, stirring occasionally, until the shallots are tender, about 5 minutes. Add the corn, hazelnuts, and salt, and cook for 2 minutes. Add the sage and cook for 1 minute more. Add the ravioli to the skillet, tossing gently to evenly coat.

Divide the pasta among the plates and top with the Asiago cheese. Serve immediately.

Note: To blanch fresh or frozen corn, bring a medium-size saucepan of cold water to a boil. Add the corn and cook until crisp-tender, 2 to 3 minutes. Remove from heat, drain, and rinse under cold water.

Note: To toast the hazelnuts, place on a baking sheet in a 350°F oven for 10 minutes, or until lightly browned and fragrant.

crab and crayfish cakes with roasted red pepper sauce

makes about 1 dozen 2-inch cakes

Crabcakes are great to serve at a party since you can prepare them hours before the guests arrive. They also make a really nice light supper with some corn on the cob and perhaps a green bean salad on the side. These are wonderful too with the Chile-Lime Mayonnaise (page 3).

¼ cup mayonnaise

¼ cup finely chopped scallions (green and white parts)

2 large eggs, lightly beaten

1½ teaspoons Dijon mustard

½ teaspoon Worcestershire sauce

¼ teaspoon Tabasco sauce

¼ teaspoon salt

¾ pound lump crab meat, picked over and flaked

½ pound frozen crayfish, defrosted

2 cups fresh coarse breadcrumbs (made from French or Italian bread)

¼ cup canola oil

2 tablespoons unsalted butter

1 recipe Roasted Red Pepper Sauce (recipe follows)

Lemon wedges, for garnish

In a large bowl, combine the mayonnaise, scallions, eggs, mustard, Worcestershire sauce, Tabasco sauce, and salt. Fold in the crab meat, crayfish, and ½ cup of the breadcrumbs. Form into 2-inch cakes, about ¾-inch thick. Heavily coat the cakes with the remaining 1½ cups breadcrumbs and transfer to a baking sheet lined with waxed paper. Chill, covered, for at least 2 hours, or overnight.

Heat 2 tablespoons of the oil with 1 tablespoon of the butter in a large skillet over medium-high heat. Add half of the crabcakes and cook until crispy and golden, about 5 minutes on each side. Add the remaining oil and butter to the skillet and cook the remaining crabcakes. Serve warm with the Roasted Red Pepper Sauce and lemon wedges.

roasted red pepper sauce

makes about 1 cup

1 cup drained, jarred roasted red peppers

1 tablespoon olive oil

1 tablespoon chopped garlic

$\frac{1}{2}$ teaspoon salt

$\frac{1}{4}$ teaspoon Tabasco sauce

$\frac{2}{3}$ cup mayonnaise

Place all the ingredients except the mayonnaise into the bowl of a food processor fitted with a steel blade and process until smooth. Transfer to a small bowl or plastic storage container. Add the mayonnaise and stir until well blended.

crostini with goat cheese, beefsteak tomatoes, and red onion

makes 6 to 8 servings

I started making these crostini years ago when I was cooking at a supper club that my family owned. They were always extremely popular, and they still are a big hit when I make them for dinner guests. You certainly don't have to use beefsteaks, but really ripe, juicy, and flavorful tomatoes are a must.

tomato and red onion topping

2 cups diced, seeded beefsteak tomatoes

1/2 cup finely chopped red onion

3 tablespoons chopped fresh basil

2 tablespoons olive oil

1 1/2 tablespoons balsamic vinegar

1/4 teaspoon salt

1/8 teaspoon freshly ground black pepper

crostini

Twenty-four 1/3-inch-thick slices French-bread baguette

6 tablespoons olive oil

2 tablespoons minced garlic

3 1/2 ounces soft fresh plain goat cheese, at room temperature

To make the tomato and red onion topping: Place all of the ingredients in a small bowl and mix together until well blended. Let stand at room temperature for about 1 hour.

Preheat the oven to 400°F.

To make the crostini: Arrange the baguette slices on a baking sheet lined with aluminum foil. In a small bowl, combine the olive oil with the garlic. Brush the top side of each baguette slice generously with the oil and garlic mixture. Bake until crisp but just lightly golden, about 12 minutes.

Remove from the oven and transfer the baguette slices to a large platter. Spread about a teaspoon of the goat cheese onto each slice and then top with about a tablespoon of the tomato-onion topping (depending on the size of your baguette, you may not use all of the topping). Serve immediately while warm.

polenta cakes with mascarpone and roasted peppers

makes 8 to 10 servings
(about 2 dozen polenta
cakes)

These make a really nice passed hors d'oeuvre since they're just the right size to pick up and eat while holding a cocktail. The polenta can be made a day in advance and then the cakes can be put together quickly . . . even with guests crowding around the kitchen.

polenta

2 cups chicken stock

2 cups whole milk

2 cups water

1 1/2 cups fresh or frozen corn kernels

1 1/2 teaspoons salt

2 cups polenta (coarse yellow cornmeal)

4 tablespoons (1/2 stick) unsalted butter, cut into small pieces

6 to 8 tablespoons olive oil

topping

1 cup mascarpone

One 7-ounce jar roasted red peppers, drained and cut into strips 2 inches long and 1/2 inch wide

To make the polenta: In a shallow Dutch oven, combine the chicken stock, milk, and water. Cover and bring to a boil over high heat. Stir in the corn and salt. Gradually whisk in the polenta. Reduce the heat to medium-low and simmer, stirring often, until the polenta is very thick, about 30 minutes. Remove from the heat and stir in the butter.

Spread the soft polenta evenly into a buttered baking sheet—it should be about 1/3 inch in thickness and probably will not cover the entire sheet. Cover tightly with plastic wrap and refrigerate for at least 4 hours, or overnight.

When completely chilled, cut the polenta into 2- to 2½-inch circles, using a round biscuit or cookie cutter. Place the polenta cakes on a second baking sheet lined with waxed paper. Heat 3 tablespoons of the oil in a large skillet over medium heat and cook about 8 of the polenta cakes until golden, 3 to 5 minutes on each side. Transfer to a baking sheet lined with paper towels and tent with foil to keep warm. Working in batches, adding oil to the skillet as you go, cook the remaining polenta cakes. Top each cake with a dollop (about 2 teaspoons) of the mascarpone and a strip of pepper. Serve immediately.

soups

butternut squash soup with apple and onion

makes 10 to 12 starter servings

This soup is quite rich, and also a bit sweet from the apples, so it is best served in small portions as an appetizer or perhaps for lunch on the side of a sandwich.

4 tablespoons (1/2 stick) unsalted butter

2 tablespoons olive oil

1 1/2 cups coarsely chopped yellow onion

3 pounds butternut squash, peeled and cut into 1-inch pieces

1 1/2 cups peeled, thickly sliced tart apples, such as Granny Smith (about 2 medium)

4 1/2 cups chicken stock

1 1/2 cups fresh apple cider

1 1/2 teaspoons salt

1/2 teaspoon white pepper

3/4 cup heavy cream

Heat the butter and oil in a heavy large pot over medium-high heat. Add the onion and cook, stirring occasionally, for 5 minutes. Add the squash and apples and continue to cook, stirring occasionally, for an additional 10 minutes. Add the chicken stock, cider, salt, and pepper. Cover and simmer gently until the squash is tender, 20 to 30 minutes. Remove from the heat and, working in batches (about 1 cup at a time), transfer the soup to a blender and purée until very smooth. Return the soup to the pot and over medium-low heat stir in the heavy cream.

yellow split pea soup with smoked ham hock

makes 4 to 6 main-dish servings

After a couple of years of tweaking the recipe, this is, quite frankly, the best pea soup I've ever eaten. It's got chunks of vegetables, great flavor from the ham hock, and everyone always loves it. Oh yes, and it's really simple to prepare too.

2 tablespoons olive oil

1 cup coarsely chopped yellow onion

1 tablespoon minced garlic

1 pound yellow split peas

1 pound carrots, cut into 1/2-inch pieces

1/4 pound celery, cut into 1/2-inch pieces

1 smoked ham hock

8 cups chicken stock

Freshly ground black pepper

Salt

Heat the oil in a heavy large pot over medium-high heat. Add the onion and garlic, reduce the heat to medium-low, and cook, stirring occasionally, until tender, 5 to 7 minutes. Add the remaining ingredients, raise the heat to high, cover, and bring to a boil. Reduce the heat to medium and simmer uncovered, stirring occasionally, until very thick and creamy, about 2 hours. Remove the ham hock, chop as much or as little of the meat as you like, and return it to the soup, discarding the bone.

Season with salt to taste. (You may not need any salt because the ham hock can be quite salty.)

tomato-lentil soup with spinach, corn, and brown rice

makes 10 main-dish servings

On a cold winter day, this hearty soup is a meal in itself—especially if you add a green salad and some nice crusty bread. This recipe makes a lot of soup, so there's plenty to freeze for another time. If I can't find nice spinach at the market, I use fresh or frozen green beans instead.

2 tablespoons unsalted butter

2 tablespoons olive oil

1 1/2 cups chopped yellow onion

1/4 cup minced garlic

1 pound carrots, cut into 1/4-inch pieces

1/4 pound celery, cut into 1/4-inch pieces

8 to 10 cups chicken stock

Two 14.5-ounce cans diced tomatoes, with juice

1 pound green lentils

Two 14.5-ounce cans tomato sauce

3/4 cup uncooked long-grain brown rice

1 tablespoon chopped fresh thyme

1 tablespoon salt

1 teaspoon ground cumin

Freshly ground black pepper

10 ounces baby spinach

1 1/2 cups frozen corn kernels

Heat the butter and oil in a heavy large pot over medium-high heat. Add the onion and garlic, reduce the heat to medium-low, and cook, stirring occasionally, until the onion is very tender, 8 to 10 minutes. Add the carrots and celery and continue to cook, stirring occasionally, for an additional 10 minutes. Add 8 cups of the chicken stock, diced tomatoes, and lentils. Cover and simmer for 1 hour. Raise the heat to high and bring to a boil. Add the tomato sauce, rice, thyme, salt, cumin, and pepper to taste. Reduce the heat back to medium-low and simmer, covered, for 30 minutes. Stir in the spinach and corn, and cook uncovered for 30 minutes more, adding more chicken stock if necessary.

cream of carrot soup

makes 8 to 10 starter servings

There's nothing like a big pot of homemade soup simmering on the stove on a chilly afternoon. This rich soup is great served as an appetizer when you're entertaining. It can be made in advance and stored in the refrigerator for up to two days.

4 1/2 cups chicken stock

1 pound carrots, cut into 1/4-inch slices

1 1/2 cups coarsely chopped yellow onion

2 tablespoons minced garlic

1 tablespoon dried basil

1 1/2 teaspoons salt

1/2 teaspoon white pepper

6 tablespoons (3/4 stick) unsalted butter

6 tablespoons all-purpose flour

3 cups whole milk

Combine the chicken stock, carrots, onion, garlic, basil, salt, and pepper in a heavy large pot over high heat. Cover and bring to a boil. Reduce the heat and simmer gently, until the carrots are tender, about 10 minutes. Remove from the heat and, working in batches (about 1 cup at a time), transfer the soup to a blender, and purée until very smooth. Set aside.

In the same pot, melt the butter over medium-high heat. When the butter is completely melted and bubbling, add the flour, whisking until well blended. Let the butter and flour cook for 3 minutes, stirring occasionally.

Meanwhile, in a separate medium-size saucepan, scald the milk (heat until just beginning to bubble on the sides of the pan). Add it to the butter and flour mixture gradually, while stirring constantly. Continue stirring until the mixture is smooth and thickened, about 5 minutes.

Return the carrot purée to the pot with the milk mixture and stir together over medium heat until heated through.

pasta e fagioli

Pasta e Fagioli soup has always been one of my favorite comfort foods. I have worked long and hard on a recipe worthy of my childhood memories, and here it is. (This is a great way to use up the small amounts of pasta you might have lying around in your cupboard—whatever kinds you use, it's important to use a variety of shapes and sizes.)

1 pound dried great northern beans

½ cup olive oil

3 cups chopped yellow onion

¼ cup minced garlic

8 to 10 cups chicken stock

Three 14.5-ounce cans diced tomatoes, with juice

¼ pound spaghetti or linguini, cooked al dente and cut into 1-inch pieces

¼ pound penne or ziti rigate, cooked al dente and cut in half

¼ pound fusilli or rotelle, cooked al dente and cut in half

1½ teaspoons dried Italian seasoning

1½ teaspoons salt

½ teaspoon freshly ground black pepper

Freshly grated Locatelli Romano cheese, for serving

Place the beans in a heavy large pot with enough cold water to cover the beans by 2 inches. Soak overnight for a minimum of 14 hours.

Drain the beans. Heat the oil in the heavy large pot over medium-high heat. Add the onion and garlic, reduce the heat to medium-low, and cook, stirring occasionally, until the onion is very tender, 8 to 10 minutes. Add 8 cups of the chicken stock, the tomatoes, and beans and raise the heat to high. Cover and bring to a boil. Reduce the heat to medium-low and simmer, covered, stirring occasionally, until the beans are very tender, about 2½ hours. Working in batches (about 1 cup at a time), purée 6 cups of the soup in the blender until smooth. Mix the purée back into the soup in the pot. Stir in the cooked pasta, Italian seasoning, salt, and pepper. Cook for 10 minutes more, uncovered, over medium-low heat, adding more chicken stock if necessary (but keep in mind that this is supposed to be a very thick soup).

Serve with a generous amount of Romano cheese. (When reheating this soup, add about ¼ cup chicken stock for each serving, because the pasta soaks up a lot of liquid.)

creamy tomato soup with orzo

makes 4 side servings

I love this recipe because it only takes about an hour to make from start to finish—a short time compared to most soup preparations—so it's perfect for when you wake up to one of those gray and dismal winter days and only grilled cheese and tomato soup will do for lunch.

2 tablespoons unsalted butter

1/2 cup chopped yellow onion

1 tablespoon minced garlic

One 28-ounce can crushed tomatoes

1 cup chicken stock

1/2 cup orzo, cooked al dente

1/2 cup heavy cream

1/2 teaspoon salt

1/4 teaspoon freshly ground black pepper

Heat the butter in a medium-size saucepan over medium-high heat. Add the onion and garlic, reduce the heat to medium-low, and cook, stirring occasionally, until the onion is very tender, 8 to 10 minutes. Add the tomatoes and chicken stock and simmer, uncovered, stirring occasionally, for 45 minutes. Remove from the heat and, working in batches (about 1 cup at a time), transfer the soup to a blender and purée until very smooth. Return the purée to the pot and stir in the orzo, cream, salt, and pepper. Cook for 10 minutes more, stirring occasionally, over medium-low heat.

lunch

pasta with garden tomatoes and fresh mozzarella

I make this pasta as soon as the first tomatoes ripen in the garden—it's really beautiful with a combination of red, yellow, and orange tomatoes. You can't beat it for a late summer afternoon lunch on the back porch. Any shape of pasta works great in this recipe, but I prefer linguini or bucatini.

1 cup olive oil

4 tablespoons (1/2 stick) unsalted butter

1 cup finely chopped Vidalia onion

1/4 cup minced garlic

1 pound pasta

4 cups coarsely chopped (1-inch chunks) and seeded vine-ripened tomatoes (see Note)

2/3 pound fresh mozzarella, cut into 1/2-inch cubes and tossed with coarse salt

3/4 cup freshly grated Locatelli Romano cheese

1/2 cup chopped fresh basil

Put a large pot of water on to boil over high heat. Heat the oil and butter in a shallow Dutch oven over medium-high heat. Add the onion and garlic, reduce the heat to medium-low, and cook, stirring occasionally, until the onion is very tender, 8 to 10 minutes. Meanwhile, add the pasta to the boiling water and cook until al dente.

Add the tomatoes to the Dutch oven, raise the heat to medium-high, and cook, stirring occasionally, until just tender, 3 to 5 minutes. Drain the pasta and add to the Dutch oven, tossing gently to evenly coat with the tomatoes. Remove from the heat and stir in the mozzarella and 1/4 cup of the Romano cheese. Transfer to a large platter and garnish with the basil and the remaining Romano cheese. Serve immediately.

Note: Be sure to thoroughly seed and remove any excess liquid from the tomatoes so it does not dilute the olive oil and change the consistency and taste of the sauce.

leek, corn, and mascarpone tart

This is my version of the popular French goat cheese tart with the Italian flavors of mascarpone and basil. I often like to make five or six 4-inch tarts instead of the one large tart—it's a little more work rolling out the dough, but it's fun to serve everyone their own individual tart.

crust

1 cup plus 2 tablespoons all-purpose flour

½ cup solid vegetable shortening

3 tablespoons ice water

filling

2 tablespoons olive oil

1½ cups sliced leeks (¼-inch pieces) (white and pale green parts only)

1½ cups fresh or frozen corn kernels

3 tablespoons chopped fresh basil

½ teaspoon salt

¼ teaspoon white pepper

1 cup mascarpone

½ cup heavy cream

2 large eggs, at room temperature

3 tablespoons finely grated Parmagiano-Reggiano cheese

Preheat the oven to 350°F.

To make the crust: Place the flour in a large bowl, and using a pastry blender, cut in the shortening until the pieces are pea-size. (If you don't have a pastry blender, my editor Justin suggests that you can also use two knives, in a crossing pattern, to cut the shortening into the flour mixture.) Sprinkle the ice water by tablespoons over the flour mixture, and toss with a fork until all the dough is moistened. Gather the dough into a ball and roll it out on a lightly floured surface to fit a 10-inch tart pan. Fit the dough into the pan and trim the edge flush with the rim. Prick all over the bottom and sides of the crust with a fork. Place the crust on a baking sheet and bake for 15 minutes. Remove from the oven and set aside.

Raise the oven temperature to 375°F.

To make the filling: Heat the oil in a large skillet over medium-high heat. Add the leeks and cook, stirring occasionally, until tender, 3 to 5 minutes. Add the corn and cook, stirring often, for 2 minutes. Stir in the basil, salt, and pepper. Remove from the heat, transfer to a large bowl, and cool for 10 minutes.

In a medium-size bowl, beat together the mascarpone, cream, and eggs until smooth, 1 to 2 minutes. Add to the leek and corn mixture and mix together until the ingredients are well blended. Transfer the filling into the crust and lightly sprinkle the Parmagiano over the top. Bake for 30 to 40 minutes, until the filling is set. Allow to cool for 10 minutes before serving.

pork loin sandwiches with arugula, roasted red peppers, and garlic-herb mayonnaise

makes 4 sandwiches

One of the things I love the most about cooking a roast is that the leftovers make delicious sandwiches for the next afternoon's lunch.

1 loaf country-style Italian or seven-grain bread

1/2 cup Garlic-Herb Mayonnaise (recipe follows)

1 pound (approximately) Mustard Herb Pork Loin Roast (page 72), cut into 1/4-inch slices

One 7-ounce jar roasted red peppers, drained and cut into 1/2-inch strips

2 cups arugula

2 tablespoons unsalted butter, at room temperature

Cut 8 slices from the loaf of bread, about 1/4 inch thick. Spread a tablespoon or more of the Garlic-Herb Mayonnaise on 4 of the slices. Top with slices of pork, red peppers, and arugula. Spread the remaining bread slices lightly with the butter and place butter side down on top of the arugula. Cut the sandwiches in half and serve.

garlic-herb mayonnaise

makes about 1 cup

1 large egg

1 tablespoon freshly squeezed lemon juice

1 tablespoon Dijon mustard

1 teaspoon minced garlic

1/4 teaspoon salt

1/8 teaspoon white pepper

1 cup olive oil

1 tablespoon chopped fresh chives

2 tablespoons chopped fresh flat-leaf parsley

In a medium-size bowl, on the medium speed of an electric hand mixer, beat the egg until lemon colored and thickened, 2 minutes. Add the lemon juice, mustard, garlic, salt, and pepper, continuing to beat until the ingredients are well blended, about 1 minute. With the mixer running, add the oil in a slow, steady stream—the mixture will become considerably thicker as you add the oil. Stir in the chives and parsley and season with additional salt to taste. The mayonnaise can be stored in the refrigerator for up to 3 days.

vegetable tacos

makes 6 servings

This is sort of a Tex-Mex open-faced taco. It's great for lunch or a casual dinner, but what I love about this recipe is that once you have the taco filling made, you're five minutes away from a delicious snack the next day.

vegetable filling

1 tablespoon unsalted butter

1 tablespoon olive oil

1/2 cup chopped yellow onion (1/4-inch dice)

1/2 cup chopped orange bell pepper (1/4-inch dice)

2 cups fresh or frozen corn kernels

1 1/2 cups diced, seeded tomatoes

1 cup chopped zucchini (1/2-inch dice)

1 teaspoon Tabasco sauce

1/4 teaspoon chili powder

Salt

tacos

2 tablespoons unsalted butter

Six 6-inch soft corn tortillas

1 1/2 cups shredded Monterey Jack cheese (4 1/2 ounces)

1 1/2 cups shredded sharp white cheddar cheese (4 1/2 ounces)

1/2 cup sour cream

1/2 cup chopped fresh cilantro

One 16-ounce package saffron yellow rice, such as Vigo, cooked according to package directions

To make the vegetable filling: Heat the butter and oil in a large skillet over medium-high heat. Add the onion, reduce the heat to medium-low, and cook, stirring occasionally, until tender, about 5 minutes. Add the pepper, and continue to cook for an additional 5 minutes. Add the corn, tomatoes, zucchini, Tabasco sauce, chili powder, and salt to taste. Raise the heat to medium-high and cook, stirring occasionally, until the vegetables are tender, 6 to 8 minutes. Remove from the heat, cover (to keep warm), and set aside.

To assemble and serve: In a second large skillet, heat 2 teaspoons of the butter over high heat. Place 2 tortillas in the skillet, and top each tortilla with a half cup of the vegetable filling and then a half cup of the mixed cheeses. Cover and cook for 2 to 4 minutes, until the cheese is melted and bubbly. Transfer the finished tacos to a platter and tent with aluminum foil to keep warm. Repeat with the remaining butter and tortillas. Serve immediately, topped with the sour cream and cilantro, with the saffron rice.

sun-dried tomato pasta salad with corn, orange pepper, and pecans

During the summer, I make this pasta salad really often for lunch. I put it all together right after breakfast, go outside to do some chores, and when I come in, lunch is ready.

½ pound rotelle or farfalle (bowtie) pasta

¼ cup olive oil

1 cup halved grape or cherry tomatoes

1 cup frozen corn kernels, defrosted

⅔ cup mayonnaise

½ cup chopped orange bell pepper

½ cup finely chopped red onion

⅓ cup Sun-Dried Tomato Pesto (recipe follows)

⅓ cup coarsely chopped toasted pecans (see Note)

¼ cup finely grated Locatelli Romano cheese

3 tablespoons chopped fresh flat-leaf parsley

Cook the pasta in a large pot of boiling water until al dente. Drain and toss with the olive oil in a large bowl or plastic food storage container.

Add the remaining ingredients and mix well. Serve at room temperature with additional Romano cheese.

Note: To toast the pecans, place on a baking sheet in a 350°F oven for 15 minutes, or until lightly browned and fragrant.

sun-dried tomato pesto

makes 1 cup

1 cup sun-dried tomatoes
(not oil packed)

1 cup olive oil

1/3 cup whole roasted almonds
(see Note)

1/4 cup freshly grated Locatelli
Romano cheese

1/4 cup loosely packed fresh basil
leaves

3 large cloves garlic

1/4 teaspoon coarse salt

I like to double or triple this recipe so that I have some on hand for pasta salads throughout the summer. Unlike regular basil pesto, this keeps really well for up to six weeks in the refrigerator.

Place all the ingredients in the bowl of a food processor fitted with a steel blade. Process until the pesto is finely puréed.

Note: To roast the almonds, place on a baking sheet in a 350°F oven for 15 minutes, or until lightly browned and fragrant.

deviled egg salad sandwiches

It's a sure sign that summer is here when we have egg salad sandwiches and lemonade for lunch on the porch. I like to make this on thinly sliced white bread.

6 hard-boiled large eggs, chopped

1 cup diced and seeded grape tomatoes

1/2 cup chopped scallions (green and white parts)

1/3 cup mayonnaise

2 tablespoons chopped fresh flat-leaf parsley

2 teaspoons Dijon mustard

1/2 teaspoon paprika

1/4 teaspoon salt

8 slices white bread

Place all the ingredients (except the bread, of course) in a medium-size bowl or plastic storage container and mix thoroughly. Serve on white bread.

risotto with peas, corn, and three cheeses

Risotto makes a great lunch, but I like to serve it as an appetizer as well. I know standing in front of the stove and stirring for half an hour isn't at the top of everyone's list, but I actually find it quite soothing. The combination of the three Italian cheeses gives this dish a more complex flavor, but if you don't have easy access to all three, using two cheeses would of course be fine.

8 cups chicken stock

2 cups water

3 tablespoons unsalted butter

3 tablespoons olive oil

1 cup finely chopped yellow onion

1/4 cup minced shallot

1 teaspoon salt

3 cups Arborio rice

3/4 cup white wine

3/4 cup frozen peas

3/4 cup frozen corn kernels

1/4 cup freshly grated Parmagiano-Reggiano cheese

1/4 cup freshly grated Locatelli Romano cheese

1/4 cup freshly grated Asiago cheese

1/4 cup chopped fresh flat-leaf parsley

Salt

White pepper

In a large saucepan, combine the chicken stock and water, bring to a low simmer, and keep warm on the stove until needed.

Heat the butter and oil in a shallow Dutch oven over medium-high heat. Add the onion, shallot, and salt, reduce the heat to medium-low and cook, stirring occasionally, until very tender, 8 to 10 minutes. Add the rice, and cook, stirring frequently, to lightly toast, 2 to 3 minutes. Add the wine and stir until it is absorbed by the rice, 1 to 2 minutes.

Begin adding the warm stock, about ½ cup at a time. Stir constantly with a wooden spoon and let each addition be absorbed before adding the next. Continue adding the stock, and stirring constantly, until the rice is tender but still al dente. This will take about 30 minutes total; you will probably not use all of the stock.

Add the peas and corn, and cook until tender, 2 to 3 minutes. Remove from the heat and stir in the three cheeses and parsley. Season with salt and white pepper to taste. Serve immediately with additional grated cheese.

turkey burgers with goat cheese and pepper & onion relish

This is a delicious alternative to regular hamburgers on the grill. I like to serve it with some red potato and haricot vert salad for a great summer meal.

burgers

1 tablespoon unsalted butter

1 tablespoon olive oil

1 cup minced yellow onion

2 pounds ground turkey breast

1 cup seasoned breadcrumbs

2 large eggs, beaten

2 tablespoons ketchup

2 teaspoons Dijon mustard

1 teaspoon garlic powder

1 teaspoon salt

$\frac{1}{2}$ teaspoon freshly ground black pepper

accompaniment

6 whole wheat sandwich buns

6 tablespoons mayonnaise

6 ounces soft, fresh plain goat cheese

1 recipe Pepper & Onion Relish (recipe follows)

To make the burgers: Heat the butter and oil in a small skillet over medium-high heat. Add the onion, reduce the heat to medium-low, and cook, stirring occasionally, until the onion is very tender, 8 to 10 minutes. Remove from the heat, transfer to a large bowl, and allow to come to room temperature. Add the remaining burger ingredients to the bowl, and blend with your hands until well combined. Divide into 6 equal portions and shape into patties.

Prepare the barbecue to medium-high heat and cover the grill with aluminum foil. Cook the burgers with the grill cover on for 5 minutes. Remove the grill cover and cook for an additional 5 minutes. Turn the burgers and cook, uncovered, for 8 to 10 minutes, until cooked through (no longer pink). Transfer to a platter and cover with aluminum foil.

Grill the burger buns, cut side down, until lightly toasted, 1 to 2 minutes.

Spread 1 tablespoon of the mayonnaise on the bottom half of each bun, and 2 tablespoons of goat cheese on the top half. Top each burger with $\frac{1}{4}$ cup of the Pepper & Onion Relish, place the burger on the bun, and serve immediately.

pepper & onion relish

makes about 1 ½ cups

3 tablespoons olive oil

1 tablespoon unsalted butter

2 cups coarsely chopped mixed yellow and red bell peppers

1 ½ cups coarsely chopped Vidalia onion

1 tablespoon minced garlic

Salt

Freshly ground black pepper

I like to use a combination of yellow and red bell peppers to make this relish colorful as well as delicious. I love it on the turkey burgers with goat cheese, but it's also delicious on a grilled chicken or steak sandwich or spread on crostini with ricotta cheese.

Heat the oil and butter in a medium-size saucepan over medium heat. Add the peppers, onion, and garlic, and cook, stirring occasionally, until very tender, about 30 minutes. Season with salt and pepper to taste. Serve warm (this can be made ahead and reheated).

weeknight dinners

meals for every day

spaghettini with summer vegetables

This is one of my favorite pasta dishes to make in the middle of the summer when all of the vegetables are fresh from the garden—it's light, flavorful, and delicious.

¾ cup olive oil

3 tablespoons unsalted butter

1 cup finely chopped Vidalia onion

3 tablespoons minced garlic

2 cups julienned carrots

1 pound spaghettini

1¼ cups julienned zucchini

1¼ cups julienned yellow summer squash

2 cups halved grape or cherry tomatoes

1½ cups fresh or frozen green peas

¼ cup freshly grated Locatelli Romano cheese, plus extra for serving

Freshly ground black pepper

Put a large pot of water on to boil over high heat. Heat the oil and butter in a shallow Dutch oven over medium-high heat. Add the onion and garlic, reduce the heat to medium-low, and cook, stirring occasionally, until the onion is very tender, 8 to 10 minutes. Add the carrots and cook until just tender, 3 to 5 minutes. Meanwhile, add the spaghettini to the boiling water and cook until al dente, 6 to 8 minutes. Add the remaining vegetables to the Dutch oven and raise the heat to medium-high, stirring occasionally, until all the vegetables are tender, about 3 minutes. Drain the spaghettini and add to the vegetables, tossing gently to evenly coat. Stir in the Romano cheese and black pepper to taste. Serve immediately with additional grated cheese.

lemon-tarragon chicken

makes 4 servings

When I lived in the city, I used to go to a little French cafe that served a chicken dish similar to this one, which I've tried to re-create at home. I like to serve it over rice pilaf to absorb all the great lemon and white wine sauce.

sauce

2 tablespoons unsalted butter

1/2 cup finely chopped yellow onion

1/4 cup minced garlic

1 cup chicken stock

1 cup white wine

1/4 cup heavy cream

1/4 cup freshly squeezed lemon juice

Salt

Freshly ground black pepper

chicken

1/4 cup all-purpose flour

1/4 teaspoon salt

Freshly ground black pepper

1 pound boneless, skinless chicken breast, cut into 2-inch pieces

2 tablespoons olive oil

1 tablespoon finely chopped fresh tarragon (or more if you like)

To make the sauce: Heat the butter in a medium-size saucepan over medium-high heat. Add the onion and garlic, reduce the heat to medium-low, and cook, stirring occasionally, until the onion is very tender, 8 to 10 minutes. Add the chicken stock and wine, raise the heat to medium-high, and gently boil, uncovered, until the liquid is reduced by half, 15 to 20 minutes.

Add the cream, lemon juice, and salt and pepper to taste, cover, and simmer for 5 minutes. Remove from the heat and set aside.

To make the chicken: In a large bowl, combine the flour with the salt and pepper to taste. Coat the chicken with the flour mixture.

Heat the oil in a large skillet over medium-high heat. Add the chicken and, stirring occasionally, sauté until golden brown and cooked through, 5 to 7 minutes. Pour the reserved sauce into the skillet with the chicken, stirring to combine and scraping up any browned bits. Stir in the tarragon and continue to cook over medium-low heat for 2 to 3 minutes.

grilled salmon with corn and cherry tomato salad

makes 6 servings

This is the perfect dinner when you're looking for a light and healthy meal on a hot summer night (and you only have to turn on the stove to blanch the corn!).

½ cup olive oil

Six 5-ounce skinless salmon filets, about 1 inch thick

Salt

Freshly ground black pepper

1 recipe Corn and Cherry Tomato Salad with Manchego Cheese (page 88)

Prepare the barbecue to medium-high heat. Brush the grilling rack with 2 tablespoons of the oil. Brush both sides of each salmon filet with the remaining olive oil and season to taste with salt and pepper. Grill for about 5 minutes on each side. Serve hot with the Corn and Cherry Tomato Salad.

baked vegetable cavatappi with *besciamella* sauce

makes 6 to 8 servings

I like to make this in the early autumn when there's just beginning to be a chill in the air and I'm craving something warm and comforting for dinner. Cauliflower is in season, and I always still have piles of tomatoes around. You can make the vegetable filling in advance and set it aside until you're ready to put together the casserole.

vegetable filling

¼ cup olive oil

2 tablespoons unsalted butter

1½ cups chopped yellow onion

¼ cup minced garlic

2 cups small cauliflower florets

1 cup thinly sliced zucchini (cut in rounds, and then cut in half again)

1 cup thinly sliced yellow summer squash (cut in rounds, and then cut in half again)

5 cups coarsely chopped, seeded tomatoes

1 teaspoon salt

½ teaspoon freshly ground black pepper

¾ cup chopped fresh basil

¼ cup chopped fresh flat-leaf parsley

1 recipe *Besciamella* Sauce (recipe follows)

1 pound cavatappi

¾ cup coarsely grated Asiago cheese

¾ cup coarsely grated Locatelli Romano cheese

Preheat the oven to 350°F.

To make the vegetable filling: Heat the oil and butter in a heavy large pot over medium-high heat. Add the onion and garlic, reduce the heat to medium-low and cook, stirring occasionally, until the onion is very tender, 8 to 10 minutes. Add the cauliflower, zucchini, and squash, raise the heat to medium, and cook, stirring occasionally, for 5 minutes. Add the tomatoes, salt, and pepper, and cook until the vegetables are just tender, about 5 minutes more. Remove from the heat and stir in the basil and parsley. (Depending upon the juiciness of your vegetables, it's a good idea to remove ¼ to ½ cup of the liquid from the pot before continuing.) Set aside.

To assemble the casserole: Bring a large pot of water to boil over high heat. Meanwhile, make the *Besciamella* Sauce. Add the cavatappi to the boiling water and cook until al dente, 7 to 9 minutes. (Remember that the noodles will continue to cook more in the oven.)

Drain the cavatappi and add to the *Besciamella* Sauce, mixing thoroughly. (Be sure to drain the pasta really well, otherwise it will thin out your sauce.) Brush the bottom of a 9 x 13 x 2-inch casserole dish with butter. Spread half of the vegetable filling over the bottom of the dish. Then spread half of the cavatappi over the vegetables and sprinkle half of the grated cheeses over the pasta. Repeat the layers and sprinkle the remaining Asiago and Romano cheeses evenly over the top of the casserole. Bake uncovered for 30 minutes.

besciamella sauce

makes about 4½ cups

½ cup (1 stick) unsalted butter, cut into pieces

½ cup all-purpose flour

2 cups whole milk

2 cups heavy cream

1 cup coarsely grated Fontina cheese (3 ounces)

½ teaspoon salt

¼ teaspoon white pepper

Melt the butter in a large saucepan over medium-high heat. When the butter is completely melted and bubbling, add the flour, whisking until well blended. Cook, stirring occasionally, for 3 minutes. Gradually add the milk and cream, whisking constantly. Bring to a boil, continuing to whisk, and cook until the sauce is smooth and thickened, 8 to 10 minutes. Stir in the Fontina, salt, and pepper. Remove from the heat.

pork cutlets with sour cream mustard sauce

makes 4 servings

This recipe was actually a bit of an accident. I asked the farmer who I get my organic meat from to pack me up some boneless pork chops to freeze for the winter, and there was a little bit of a misunderstanding, and I wound up with pork cutlets. I made this dish and it's now one of our favorites—and a really nice change from chicken.

pork

Four ¼-inch-thick pork cutlets
(or boneless thin-cut pork chops)

2 cups whole milk

2 teaspoons salt

3½ cups fresh coarse white
breadcrumbs

3 tablespoons minced garlic

2 tablespoons finely chopped
fresh chives

1 tablespoon finely chopped fresh
flat-leaf parsley

¼ cup olive oil

2 tablespoons unsalted butter

sour cream mustard sauce

1½ cups sour cream
(do not use reduced-fat sour cream)

1½ cups chicken stock

3 tablespoons whole grain Dijon
mustard

1 tablespoon Dijon mustard

1 tablespoon cornstarch

Place the pork cutlets with the milk and salt in a shallow casserole dish. Cover and refrigerate for 2 hours (1 hour is okay if you're short on time).

In a medium-size bowl, combine the breadcrumbs with the garlic, chives, and parsley. Lift the pork chops out of the milk, one at a time, coat each side very heavily with the breadcrumb mixture (pat in with your hands if necessary), and transfer to a large plate.

Heat 2 tablespoons of the oil with 1 tablespoon of the butter in a large skillet over medium-high heat. Add 2 of the cutlets and cook until crisp, golden, and no longer pink inside, about 4 minutes on each side. Transfer the cutlets, as cooked, to a large plate and tent with foil to keep warm. Add the remaining oil and butter to the skillet and cook the remaining cutlets. While cooking the cutlets, make the sauce.

To make the sour cream mustard sauce: Place all of the ingredients in a medium-size saucepan and whisk together over medium heat, until well blended. Simmer, stirring occasionally, until slightly thickened, about 5 minutes. Cover, remove from the heat, and set aside. (The sauce will continue to thicken while sitting.)

Transfer the pork cutlets to plates, spoon the mustard sauce on top, and serve.

chicken and broccoli au gratin

My mom started making this many years ago, after enjoying a similar dish at a restaurant. You can make this dinner any night of the week very easily by either roasting the chicken the night before, or picking up a rotisserie chicken from the local market. I like to serve this casserole with long-grain brown rice.

2 whole (4 split) chicken breasts (bone in, skin on)

3 tablespoons olive oil

1 pound broccoli, cut into 1-inch pieces (about 4 cups)

white sauce

4 tablespoons (½ stick) unsalted butter

¼ cup all-purpose flour

2 cups whole milk

¾ cup shredded sharp white cheddar cheese (about 2 ounces)

¾ cup shredded Monterey Jack cheese (about 2 ounces)

1 teaspoon salt

¼ teaspoon white pepper

Preheat the oven to 375°F.

Place the chicken breasts in a large glass baking dish, skin side up, and brush with the olive oil. Roast for 35 to 40 minutes, or until the chicken is cooked through. Remove from the oven and set aside to cool to room temperature, about 30 minutes. Lower the oven temperature to 350°F. Remove the meat from the bones, discard the skin, and shred the chicken into strips about 2 inches long and ½ inch wide. (You should have about 4 cups of chicken.)

Steam the broccoli over boiling water until just tender, 4 to 5 minutes.

Place the chicken in a 2-quart casserole dish. Spread the broccoli over the chicken. Set aside.

To make the white sauce: Melt the butter in the top of a double boiler, over boiling water. When the butter is completely melted and bubbling, add the flour, whisking until well blended. Cook, stirring occasionally, for 3 minutes.

Meanwhile, in a separate small saucepan, scald the milk (heat until just beginning to bubble on the sides of the pan). Add the milk to the butter-and-flour mixture gradually, while stirring constantly. Continue stirring until the sauce is smooth and thickened, about 5 minutes. Stir in the cheeses, salt, and pepper. Remove from the heat and pour the sauce evenly over the top of the chicken and broccoli. Bake uncovered for 30 minutes.

gemelli with sun-dried tomatoes, artichokes, arugula, and yellow pepper

makes 6 servings

The first time I made this pasta was when I was still working extremely long hours at the bakery and would come home and cook up a late-night dinner with whatever I happened to have in the fridge. This turned out quite well for a midnight snack, and I've been making it ever since.

½ cup olive oil

2 tablespoons unsalted butter

1 cup finely chopped yellow onion

¼ cup minced garlic

1½ cups coarsely chopped yellow bell pepper

1 pound gemelli or other shaped pasta

2 cups coarsely chopped (1-inch chunks), seeded, vine-ripened tomatoes

Two 6-ounce jars marinated artichoke hearts, well drained and cut in half (about 2 cups)

6 ounces baby arugula

1 cup jarred sun-dried tomatoes in oil, lightly drained

1 cup heavy cream

¼ cup freshly grated Locatelli Romano cheese, plus extra for serving

1 teaspoon salt

½ teaspoon freshly ground black pepper

½ cup mascarpone cheese, for garnish

⅓ cup chopped fresh basil, for garnish

Put a large pot of water on to boil over high heat.

Heat the oil with the butter in a shallow Dutch oven over medium-high heat. Add the onion and garlic, reduce the heat to medium-low, and cook, stirring occasionally, until the onion is very tender, 8 to 10 minutes. Add the pepper and cook, still stirring occasionally, until just tender, about 2 minutes.

Meanwhile, add the gemelli to the boiling water and cook until al dente, about 7 minutes.

Add the remaining vegetables to the Dutch oven, raise the heat to medium, and cook, stirring often, until the tomatoes are tender and the arugula is wilted, about 5 minutes.

Add the sun-dried tomatoes, cream, Romano cheese, salt, and pepper to the Dutch oven, and cook, stirring to incorporate, for about 2 minutes.

Drain the gemelli and add to the vegetables and sauce, tossing gently to evenly coat. Divide the pasta among six plates, and top each with a dollop (about a tablespoon) of the mascarpone and a sprinkle of the chopped basil. Serve immediately with additional grated cheese.

old-fashioned meatloaf

makes 4 to 6 servings

After spending an afternoon enjoying the first crisp day in autumn, there's nothing like a hearty meatloaf for dinner. As far as I'm concerned, one must serve meatloaf with mashed potatoes. (And Brussels sprouts.) (And corn.)

1 1/2 pounds ground meat (Have your butcher prepare a mixture of 1/2 pound beef, 1/2 pound pork, and 1/2 pound veal if not available at your local grocery.)

1 cup finely chopped yellow onion

1/2 cup seasoned breadcrumbs

1/2 cup ketchup

2 large eggs, beaten

2 tablespoons Worcestershire sauce

1 tablespoon dried basil

2 teaspoons garlic powder

1 teaspoon salt

1/2 teaspoon freshly ground black pepper

Preheat the oven to 350°F.

Place all the ingredients in a large bowl and blend with your hands until well combined. Transfer the meat mixture into a 9 x 5½ x 3-inch glass loaf pan. Bake for 45 to 50 minutes, or until desired doneness.

halibut with horseradish crust

This is another recipe from my friend Dave Cole, who owns Dave's Big Eddy Diner, near my home in upstate New York. It took me a year to finally get him sitting on my living room couch with a glass of wine and a pen and paper, but it was certainly worth the wait. If you have trouble finding halibut at the market, you could substitute cod instead.

6 tablespoons ($^3/_4$ stick) unsalted butter

$^3/_4$ cup minced yellow onion

$^3/_4$ cup plain breadcrumbs, fresh if possible

3 tablespoons prepared horseradish

Four 6-ounce skinless halibut filets

Salt

Freshly ground black pepper

Preheat the oven to 425°F.

Melt the butter in a small skillet over medium-high heat. Add the onion, reduce the heat to medium, and cook, stirring occasionally, until the onion is lightly brown and tender, about 8 minutes. Remove from the heat and add the breadcrumbs and horseradish, stirring to incorporate. Set aside.

Season the halibut filets with salt and pepper to taste and place in a large, shallow casserole dish. Top each filet with an equal amount of the breadcrumb mixture, pressing lightly to adhere. Bake for 12 to 15 minutes, until the crust is golden and the fish is opaque.

three-can tuna casserole

makes 4 servings

I think tuna casserole might be the ultimate comfort food. Everyone has those days when they come home late from work and a healthy, well balanced meal is just not going to make it onto the dinner table. I always seem to make this on gloomy, rainy evenings, and then I curl up on the couch in front of the television. (And then I make some good, old-fashioned My-T-Fine chocolate pudding for dessert.)

½ pound broad egg noodles

One 10½-ounce can Campbell's Cream of Celery soup

½ cup milk

One 8-ounce package cream cheese, cut into ½-inch cubes

One 12-ounce can solid white albacore tuna in water, drained

One 11-ounce can vacuum-packed sweet corn, drained

¼ cup plain breadcrumbs

1 tablespoon freshly grated Locatelli Romano or Parmagiano-Reggiano cheese

Preheat the oven to 375°F.

Cook the egg noodles according to the package directions, being careful not to overcook. Drain and set aside.

In a large bowl, stir together the soup, milk, and half of the cream cheese until well blended. Add the tuna, corn, and noodles and mix thoroughly. Add the remaining cream cheese and mix just to distribute the cubes evenly throughout. Transfer to a 2-quart casserole dish. Sprinkle with the breadcrumbs and cheese. Bake uncovered for 25 minutes.

cavatelli with turkey sausage, tomato, and broccoli rabe

You'll find cavatelli pasta in the frozen foods section of your grocery store with the ravioli. Many people have never tasted cavatelli, and it really has a taste and texture all its own. For this pasta dish, I took two traditionally paired ingredients—sausage and broccoli rabe—but changed it up a bit using turkey sausage and adding just a bit of tomato.

1 pound broccoli rabe, coarsely chopped (2- to 3-inch pieces are good)

6 tablespoons olive oil

¾ pound sweet Italian turkey sausage, casings removed

¼ cup minced garlic

2 pounds frozen ricotta cavatelli

1 cup canned crushed tomatoes

1 teaspoon salt

Finely grated Parmagiano-Reggiano cheese

Freshly ground black pepper

Put a large pot of water on to boil over high heat. Bring a second large saucepan of water to boil. Add the broccoli rabe to the saucepan and cook until crisp-tender, 2 minutes. Remove from the heat, drain, and plunge the broccoli rabe into a large bowl of cold water. Transfer to a salad spinner and spin dry. Set aside.

Heat 3 tablespoons of the olive oil in a shallow Dutch oven, over medium-high heat. Add the sausage, breaking it up with a wooden spoon and stirring often, until the sausage is in small pieces and is thoroughly cooked through, about 5 minutes. Reduce the heat to medium-low and stir in the garlic.

Meanwhile, add the cavatelli to the pot of boiling water and cook according to the package directions, 5 to 7 minutes. Add the crushed tomatoes and the salt to the Dutch oven and cook, stirring occasionally, for 5 minutes. Drain the cavatelli and add to the Dutch oven with the broccoli rabe and remaining 3 tablespoons of olive oil, tossing gently to evenly coat. Cook for 2 minutes more.

Serve immediately with grated Parmagiano cheese and black pepper to taste.

chicken with mustard-shallot cream sauce

makes 4 servings

This is one of my favorite chicken dishes. It's easy enough to prepare any night of the week, but definitely special enough to entertain with.

mustard-shallot cream sauce

1/2 cup minced shallots

3/4 cup white wine

1 1/2 cups heavy cream

2 tablespoons whole grain Dijon mustard

2 tablespoons Dijon mustard

chicken

1/4 cup all-purpose flour

1/4 teaspoon salt

Freshly ground black pepper

1 pound boneless, skinless chicken breast, cut into 1-inch pieces

2 tablespoons olive oil

1 tablespoon unsalted butter

To make the mustard-shallot cream sauce: In a medium-size saucepan, combine the shallots and wine and bring to a boil over high heat. Reduce the heat to medium-high and gently boil, uncovered, until the wine is reduced by half, 5 to 7 minutes. Stir in the cream, cover, reduce the heat to medium, and simmer for 5 minutes. Stir in the mustards and cook for 2 minutes more. Remove from the heat and set aside.

To make the chicken: In a large bowl, combine the flour with the salt and pepper to taste. Coat the chicken with the flour mixture. Heat the oil and butter in a large skillet over medium-high heat. Add the chicken and sauté, stirring occasionally, until golden brown and cooked through, about 5 minutes.

Pour the reserved sauce into the skillet with the chicken and continue to cook over medium-low heat for 2 to 3 minutes. Season with additional salt and pepper to taste.

weekend dinners
meals for entertaining

chicken and vegetable stew with cream cheese herb crust

makes enough filling for two
9-inch pies or 6 to 8 servings

I've always wanted to come up with an easier version of chicken pot pie, or chicken stew, that didn't require poaching or roasting the chicken, and separate pots for every step. This recipe makes enough filling for two pies, so what I do quite often is freeze the second half of the stew for another time, and then I only need to defrost it and make the crust and I'm all set for dinner.

stew

2 tablespoons olive oil

1 pound boneless, skinless chicken breast, cut into 1-inch pieces

1/2 pound carrots, cut into 1/4-inch pieces

1/4 pound parsnips, cut into 1/4-inch pieces

1/2 cup (1 stick) unsalted butter

1 1/2 cups coarsely chopped yellow onion

3 tablespoons minced garlic

1/2 cup all-purpose flour

3 cups chicken stock, at room temperature

3 tablespoons heavy cream

3 tablespoons chopped fresh flat-leaf parsley

2 tablespoons finely chopped fresh chives

1 1/2 teaspoons salt

1/2 teaspoon white pepper

1 cup frozen peas

1 cup frozen corn kernels

To make the stew: Heat the oil in a heavy large pot over medium-high heat. Add the chicken and cook, stirring occasionally, until cooked through, about 5 minutes. Remove from the heat. Transfer the chicken to a bowl and set aside.

Bring a medium saucepan of cold water to a boil. Add the carrots and parsnips, cover, and cook until crisp-tender, 3 to 4 minutes. Remove from the heat, drain, and set aside.

Preheat the oven to 375°F.

In the same heavy large pot that you cooked the chicken in, melt the butter over medium heat. Add the onion and garlic, and cook, stirring occasionally, until the onion is very tender, 8 to 10 minutes. Add the flour, and cook, stirring often, for 3 minutes. Add the chicken stock and cream, bring to a simmer over medium heat, and continue to simmer, uncovered, stirring occasionally, until thickened, about 8 minutes. Add the parsley, chives, salt, and pepper and remove from the heat. Stir in the reserved chicken and vegetables and the peas and corn. Set aside.

To make the crust: Place the flour, thyme, and salt in a large bowl. Using a pastry blender, cut in the butter and cream cheese until the pieces are pea-size. (If you don't have a pastry blender, my editor Justin suggests that you can also use two knives, in a crossing pattern, to cut the butter into

crust (for one 9-inch pie—double the measurements if making 2 pies)

1 1/4 cups all-purpose flour

1 teaspoon finely chopped fresh thyme

1/4 teaspoon salt

1/2 cup (1 stick) unsalted butter, softened and cut into small pieces

4 ounces (half an 8-ounce package) cream cheese, softened and cut into small pieces

1 large egg, beaten, for egg wash

the flour mixture.) Gather the dough into a ball (it will seem very crumbly but be patient with it), and roll out on a lightly floured surface to fit a 9-inch glass pie dish. Set aside.

Spoon half of the stew into the pie dish. Place the crust over the filling, trim the edges of the dough, and crimp. Lightly brush the crust with the egg (just lightly brush—you will not use most of the egg). Make several 1-inch steam slits in the center of the crust with the tip of a paring knife.

Place the pie dish on a baking sheet and bake for 40 to 50 minutes, until the crust is golden.

traditional bolognese lasagne

makes 6 to 8 servings

This traditional Italian-style lasagne has no mozzarella or ricotta cheeses, but with the delicious creamy *besciamella*, you won't miss them at all. It is my absolute favorite baked pasta dish and a very comforting dinner on a winter evening.

One 12-ounce box (³⁄₄ pound) rippled edge lasagne noodles (not oven-ready lasagne)

1 recipe Bolognese Sauce (recipe follows)

1 recipe *Besciamella* Sauce (page 49), omitting the 1 cup Fontina cheese and allowing the sauce to stand at room temperature for 10 minutes before assembling the lasagne

¹⁄₂ cup finely grated Locatelli Romano cheese

Preheat the oven to 350°F.

Bring a large pot of water to boil over high heat. Add the lasagne noodles, stirring gently to prevent them from sticking together. Continue to boil, stirring occasionally, until the lasagne is tender, but still quite al dente, 4 to 5 minutes. (Remember that the noodles will continue to cook more in the oven.)

Drain well and spread the noodles in a single layer on waxed paper to cool slightly.

Brush the bottom of a 9 x 13 x 2-inch casserole dish with butter. Place a layer of lasagne noodles over the bottom of the dish, overlapping the noodles. Spread a layer of the Bolognese Sauce (about 2 cups) over the noodles, and then a layer of the *Besciamella* Sauce (about 1½ cups). Repeat the layers twice more, using only 1 cup of Bolognese for the top layer and being sure to end with the *Besciamella* Sauce. Sprinkle the Romano cheese evenly over the top of the casserole. Bake uncovered for 30 minutes.

bolognese sauce

makes 5½ cups (enough for about 1½ pounds of pasta)

⅓ cup olive oil

½ cup finely chopped yellow onion

2 tablespoons minced garlic

⅔ cup finely chopped carrots

⅓ cup finely chopped zucchini

⅓ cup finely chopped yellow summer squash

½ pound ground meat (Have your butcher prepare a mixture of ¼ pound beef, ⅛ pound pork, and ⅛ pound veal, if not available at your local grocery.)

3 tablespoons heavy cream

One 28-ounce can crushed tomatoes

One 6-ounce can tomato paste

¾ teaspoon salt

¼ teaspoon freshly ground black pepper

2 tablespoons chopped fresh basil

Many people think that meat sauce and Bolognese sauce are the very same thing, but the Bolognese has vegetables and a touch of cream, which gives it a more complex flavor.

Heat the oil in a heavy large pot over medium-high heat. Add the onion and garlic, reduce the heat to medium-low, and cook, stirring occasionally, until the onion is very tender, 8 to 10 minutes. Add the carrots, zucchini, and squash, and cook until tender, 4 to 5 minutes. Add the ground meat, raise the heat to medium-high, and continue to cook, breaking up the meat with a wooden spoon and stirring often, until the meat is browned through, about 5 minutes. Reduce the heat to medium-low and add 2 tablespoons of the cream, stirring until well combined. Add the crushed tomatoes, tomato paste, salt, and pepper, and simmer, uncovered, for 45 minutes. Stir in the remaining 1 tablespoon of heavy cream and the basil. Use immediately or store, covered, in the refrigerator, for up to 3 days.

baked flounder with tomato and basil cream

This is one of those great recipes that I've been making for years—a really lovely fish that's simple to prepare and never disappoints.

tomato and basil cream

2 cups diced, seeded, vine-ripened tomatoes

6 tablespoons olive oil

$1/4$ cup minced shallots

$1/4$ cup chopped fresh basil

$1/4$ cup freshly squeezed lemon juice

$1/2$ teaspoon salt

$1/4$ teaspoon freshly ground black pepper

1 cup heavy cream

2 tablespoons white wine

flounder

Four 5- to 6-ounce flounder filets

$1/4$ cup olive oil

To make the tomato and basil cream: In a medium-size bowl, combine the tomatoes, olive oil, shallots, basil, lemon juice, salt, and pepper. Cover and let stand at room temperature for 1 hour (or up to 6 hours).

Preheat the oven to 450°F.

In a medium-size saucepan, combine the cream and wine and bring to a boil, uncovered, over high heat. Reduce the heat to medium and simmer for 3 minutes. Remove from the heat, add the reserved tomato-basil mixture, cover, and set aside.

To make the flounder: Brush both sides of each flounder filet with the ¼ cup of olive oil and place in a large, shallow casserole dish. Bake uncovered for 8 to 10 minutes, or until the fish is opaque. Remove from the oven and pour the Tomato and Basil Cream sauce evenly over the fish in the casserole dish. Serve immediately.

roast lemon herb chicken with pan juices

makes 4 servings

I know that everyone has their favorite recipe for roast chicken and that every cookbook has one as well. I guess it's because it's one of those wonderful traditional meals that we all think of when we think of home cooking. I love this recipe because it's an extremely simple, juicy, and flavorful roast chicken. And since it's served in its own juices, there's no need to make gravy. (If I'm having six or eight people for dinner, or if I want a lot of leftovers for chicken salad, I just buy two chickens and double the rest of the ingredients.)

One 3- to 4-pound roasting chicken

3 tablespoons olive oil

1 tablespoon finely chopped fresh tarragon

1 ½ teaspoons finely chopped fresh thyme

Salt

Freshly ground black pepper

¾ cup white wine

¾ cup chicken stock

¼ cup freshly squeezed lemon juice

Preheat the oven to 425°F.

Remove the neck and giblets from the chicken. Rinse the chicken with cold water, inside and out, and pat dry with paper towels. Place the chicken, breast side up, on a rack in a roasting pan. Brush the chicken with the olive oil. Sprinkle evenly with the herbs, and salt and pepper to taste.

Roast the chicken uncovered for 30 minutes. Remove from the oven and turn the temperature down to 375°F. Pour the white wine, chicken stock, and lemon juice over the chicken. Return to the oven and roast, uncovered, basting every 20 minutes, for approximately 1 hour, or until the drumsticks move easily in their sockets and a meat thermometer registers 180°F when inserted into the outer thigh.

Remove the chicken from the oven and transfer to a carving board. Cover loosely with aluminum foil and allow to rest for 15 to 20 minutes before carving. Serve with the pan juices.

potato gnocchi with tomato cream sauce, peas, and mozzarella

makes 6 servings

Making gnocchi at home can seem a bit daunting, but it's really not difficult and the results are well worth the effort. You can make the mashed potatoes a day in advance—just bring them to room temperature before proceeding with the recipe.

mashed potatoes

2 1/2 pounds russet potatoes, peeled and cut into 1/2-inch slices

1 cup half-and-half

4 tablespoons (1/2 stick) unsalted butter, cut into pieces

1/2 teaspoon salt

Freshly ground black pepper

gnocchi

3 large egg yolks

6 tablespoons olive oil

2 1/2 cups all-purpose flour

1 teaspoon salt

1 1/2 cups frozen green peas

1 recipe Tomato Cream Sauce (recipe follows)

1/2 pound mozzarella cheese, cut into 1/2-inch cubes

To make the mashed potatoes: Put the potatoes in a large saucepan and cover with cold water by about 1 inch. Bring to a boil, cover the pot partially, and lower the heat to maintain a steady simmer. Cook until the potatoes are very tender when pierced with a fork, about 10 minutes. Drain, return to the saucepan, and reduce the heat to low. Using a hand masher, mash until smooth. Stir in the half-and-half, butter, salt, and pepper. Remove from the heat, transfer to a large bowl, and allow to cool to room temperature.

To make the gnocchi: In a bowl, beat together the egg yolks and olive oil. Add to the cooled potatoes with the flour and salt and gently mix together until well incorporated.

To form the gnocchi, break off pieces of dough about 1/2 cup in volume. With floured hands, gently roll the dough into cylinders about 3/4 inch in diameter. Lay the cylinders on a floured surface and, using a sharp knife, cut into 1-inch pieces. Lay the finished gnocchi on a baking sheet lined with waxed paper, keeping them separate to prevent them from sticking together. Let stand for 10 to 15 minutes.

Bring a large pot of water to a boil. Gently drop one quarter of the gnocchi into the water, and cook until the gnocchi float to the surface, 3 to 5 minutes. Using a slotted spoon, transfer the gnocchi to a colander set over a bowl. Repeat with the remaining gnocchi.

Add the peas to the pot and cook until crisp-tender, 2 to 3 minutes. Remove from the heat and drain. Transfer the gnocchi to a bowl and gently toss with the Tomato Cream Sauce, peas, and mozzarella cheese. Serve immediately.

tomato cream sauce

makes 4 cups (enough for about 1 pound of pasta)

1/3 cup olive oil

1 tablespoon unsalted butter

1 cup finely chopped Vidalia onion

2 tablespoons minced garlic

One 28-ounce can crushed tomatoes

3/4 teaspoon salt

1/4 teaspoon freshly ground black pepper

1/2 cup heavy cream

2 tablespoons freshly grated Locatelli Romano cheese

Heat the oil and butter in a heavy large pot over medium-high heat. Add the onion and garlic, reduce the heat to medium-low and cook, stirring occasionally, until the onion is very tender, 8 to 10 minutes. Add the tomatoes, salt, and pepper and simmer, uncovered, stirring occasionally, for 30 minutes. Stir in the cream and Romano cheese. Use immediately or store, covered, in the refrigerator for up to 3 days.

mustard herb pork loin roast with cornbread apple-pecan dressing and cider gravy

makes 6 to 8 servings

It's nice to invite friends who live in the city up for a weekend in early October when the autumn colors are at their prettiest. It is also the time when I'm getting excited about cooking foods that we haven't eaten since last year. Roasts are great to serve at dinner parties—they're so easy to prepare and they always make a nice presentation. Don't forget that you need to make the corn muffins for the dressing at least one day in advance.

makes 6 to 8 servings

pork

3 tablespoons coarse grain Dijon mustard

3 tablespoons Dijon mustard

2 tablespoons olive oil

2 tablespoons balsamic vinegar

2 tablespoons minced garlic

1 teaspoon finely chopped fresh sage

1 teaspoon finely chopped fresh thyme

One 2½- to 3-pound boneless pork loin, trimmed and tied

Salt

Freshly ground black pepper

1 recipe Cornbread Apple-Pecan Dressing (page 84)

cider gravy

3 tablespoons unsalted butter

⅓ cup minced shallots

3 tablespoons unbleached flour

1½ cups chicken stock

1½ cups apple cider

Salt

Freshly ground black pepper

Preheat the oven to 375°F.

To make the pork: In a small bowl, combine the mustards, oil, vinegar, garlic, sage, and thyme. Pat the pork loin dry with paper towels. Season with salt and pepper to taste. Coat the pork with the mustard mixture and then place on a rack in a roasting pan. Allow it to sit at room temperature for 45 minutes. Roast, uncovered, for approximately 1 hour and 15 minutes.

Meanwhile, prepare the cornbread dressing. You can put the dressing in the oven about half an hour after the pork goes in.

When a meat thermometer inserted into the center of the pork registers 140°F, remove the pork from the oven and transfer to a carving board. Cover loosely with aluminum foil, and allow to rest for 15 to 20 minutes.

To make the cider gravy: Melt the butter in a medium-size saucepan over medium heat. Add the shallots and cook, stirring occasionally, until tender, about 5 minutes. Add the flour and cook, stirring often, for 2 minutes more. Add the stock and cider, raise the heat to medium-high, and simmer for 10 minutes, whisking occasionally. Season with salt and pepper to taste.

Remove the cornbread dressing from the oven. Remove the strings from the pork, slice it thickly, and serve with the dressing and gravy.

chicken kiev

makes 4 servings

Chicken Kiev was always one of my favorite meals as a child. I remember making it with my mom on special occasions. It's one of those tasty dishes that no one seems to make anymore, and I'm not sure why.

5 tablespoons salted butter, softened

1 tablespoon freshly squeezed lemon juice

1 tablespoon minced garlic

1 teaspoon finely chopped fresh flat-leaf parsley

4 boneless, skinless chicken breasts (about 1 1/2 pounds total)

1 large egg

2 tablespoons water

1/2 teaspoon salt

1/4 teaspoon freshly ground black pepper

2/3 cup seasoned breadcrumbs

1/3 cup wheat germ

1/2 cup all-purpose flour

3 tablespoons olive oil

1 tablespoon salted butter

In a small bowl, beat together the softened butter, lemon juice, garlic, and parsley. Divide the butter mixture into 4 small egg-shaped pieces. Place in a plastic food storage container and chill for at least 2 hours.

Preheat the oven to 350°F.

Place each chicken breast half between 2 pieces of waxed paper. Pound the breasts lightly into a rectangle about 1/4 inch thick. Remove the waxed paper.

Put 1 piece of the butter mixture in the center of each chicken breast. Fold in the sides of the chicken, then roll up from one of the short ends, securing with wooden toothpicks as needed. (I find that it is best to use the same number of toothpicks in each chicken roll so that you remember to take all of them out of each piece before serving.)

In a shallow dish, beat together the egg, water, salt, and pepper. In a second shallow dish, combine the breadcrumbs and wheat germ. In a third dish, place the flour. Coat the chicken rolls first in the flour, then dip in the egg mixture, and then in the breadcrumb mixture, being sure to coat all of the sides.

Heat the oil and butter in a large skillet over medium-high heat. Add the chicken and cook 1 to 2 minutes on all sides, until golden brown. To make this easier to do, be sure that all of the toothpicks are pushed into the chicken as far as possible. Remove the chicken from the skillet, place in a casserole dish, and bake, covered, for 25 minutes or until the chicken is tender and no longer pink inside. Be sure to remove the toothpicks before serving.

vegetable and beef stew

makes 6 servings

I'm a big fan of stew on a cold winter evening, but I go heavy on the vegetables and lighter on the meat for a healthier, more well-rounded meal. This stew is perfect served on top of buttered noodles with scallions and Parmagiano and with just a dollop of sour cream.

stew

1 pound boneless beef chuck roast, cut into 1-inch pieces

1/2 cup all-purpose flour

1 tablespoon sweet Hungarian paprika

1/2 teaspoon salt

1/4 teaspoon freshly ground black pepper

1/4 cup olive oil

1/4 cup minced garlic

3 cups red wine

One 14-ounce can tomato sauce

One 6-ounce can tomato paste

1 pound potatoes (any type is fine), unpeeled and cut into 1/2-inch chunks

1 pound carrots cut into 1/2-inch chunks

1 large yellow onion (about 1/2 pound), peeled and quartered

3 cups frozen green peas

accompaniment

1 pound egg noodles (I really love to use egg bowties)

6 tablespoons (3/4 stick) butter

1/2 cup chopped scallions (green parts only)

Preheat the oven to 300°F.

In a large bowl, toss the beef with the flour, paprika, salt, and pepper.

Heat the oil in a large Dutch oven over medium heat. Add the garlic and beef (with any extra flour) and gently brown the meat, stirring occasionally, for 3 to 5 minutes. Return the beef to the bowl and set aside.

Add the red wine, tomato sauce, and tomato paste to the Dutch oven, whisking to combine. Cook over medium-low heat, stirring constantly, for 5 minutes.

Remove from the heat, and stir in the beef, potatoes, carrots, and onion. Place in the oven, covered, and cook for 3½ hours, stirring occasionally (about once every 45 minutes is fine). Add the peas and cook, covered, for an additional half hour.

Put a large pot of water on to boil over high heat. Cook the noodles according to the package directions, being careful not to overcook. Drain the noodles and return to the pot with the butter, scallions, and Parmagiano-Reggiano cheese, tossing gently to evenly coat.

Remove the stew from the oven and serve over the egg noodles. Top with the sour cream and parsley.

⅓ cup finely grated Parmagiano-Reggiano cheese

¾ cup sour cream

2 tablespoons chopped fresh flat-leaf parsley

bucatini with chicken, hickory bacon, orange pepper, and pesto

makes 4 to 6 servings

My boyfriend, Tadhg, has been making some version of this pasta for years in the many places he's lived around the world. He tends to change it a little bit pretty much every time he makes it, and to put in whatever he sees around the kitchen, so it was quite difficult to pin down an actual recipe. It might seem to have some incongruous ingredients for a pasta dish, but it's incredibly flavorful and delicious.

chicken

½ pound boneless, skinless chicken breast, cut into 1-inch pieces

1 tablespoon olive oil

1 tablespoon white wine

½ teaspoon dried Italian seasoning

½ teaspoon chili powder

½ teaspoon coriander

1 teaspoon minced fresh ginger

pasta

8 slices hickory smoked bacon, chopped (½-inch pieces)

⅓ cup olive oil

2 tablespoons unsalted butter

1 cup finely chopped red onion

3 tablespoons minced garlic

1 pound bucatini (or linguini)

1 cup coarsely chopped orange bell pepper

¾ cup frozen corn kernels

5 ounces baby spinach

1¼ cups heavy cream

To marinate the chicken: In a medium-size bowl, combine the chicken with the olive oil, wine, Italian seasoning, chili powder, and coriander. Cover tightly with plastic wrap and place in the refrigerator for 1 to 2 hours.

Put a large pot of water on to boil over high heat.

Place the marinated chicken with the ginger in a medium skillet over medium-high heat and cook, stirring occasionally, until cooked through, about 5 minutes. Remove from the heat. Transfer the chicken to a bowl and set aside.

To make the pasta: In the same skillet, over medium heat, cook the bacon until browned but not crispy, about 10 minutes. Remove from the heat, remove the bacon from the pan with a slotted spoon, and set aside.

Heat the ⅓ cup oil with the butter in a shallow Dutch oven over medium-high heat. Add the onion and garlic, reduce the heat to medium-low and cook, stirring occasionally, until the onion is very tender, 8 to 10 minutes.

Meanwhile, add the bucatini to the boiling water and cook until al dente, 10 to 12 minutes.

Add the pepper, corn, and spinach to the Dutch oven, and cook until the pepper is just tender and the spinach is wilted, 2 to 3 minutes. Add the

2/3 cup Pesto (recipe follows)

1/2 cup toasted pine nuts (see Note)

1/4 cup finely grated Locatelli Romano cheese

cream, Pesto, pine nuts, and Romano cheese to the Dutch oven and cook for 3 more minutes, stirring to incorporate. Drain the bucatini and add to the vegetables and sauce with the reserved chicken and bacon, tossing gently to blend all of the ingredients. Serve immediately with additional grated cheese.

Note: To toast the pine nuts, place on a baking sheet in a 350°F oven for 12 minutes, or until lightly browned and fragrant.

pesto

makes about 1 1/2 cups

3 cups loosely packed basil leaves

1 cup olive oil

1/4 cup freshly grated Locatelli Romano cheese

1/4 cup toasted pine nuts (see Note)

1/4 cup chopped toasted walnuts (see Note)

3 large garlic cloves

1/2 teaspoon coarse salt

Anyone who has a vegetable garden usually makes big batches of pesto all summer long. I like to freeze it in tiny plastic storage containers (a little goes a long way in most recipes!) to use in the winter months when basil is not so readily available.

Place all the ingredients in a blender and process until the pesto is finely puréed. Use immediately, or store in the refrigerator with a thin film of olive oil on top, covered, for up to 24 hours.

Note: To toast the nuts, place on a baking sheet in a 350°F oven for 12 minutes, or until lightly browned and fragrant.

sides and casseroles

summer squash and sweet corn casserole

This is my version of a Southern classic. It's a great way to use up some of that extra squash you have in your vegetable garden by the middle of the summer.

breadcrumb topping

1 tablespoon olive oil

2 teaspoons unsalted butter

2 tablespoons minced garlic

1 cup fresh breadcrumbs

squash filling

1 tablespoon olive oil

1 tablespoon unsalted butter

1 $\frac{1}{2}$ cups chopped yellow onion

4 cups thinly sliced ($\frac{1}{4}$ inch thick) yellow summer squash

1 cup fresh or frozen corn kernels

1 cup shredded sharp white cheddar cheese (3 ounces)

$\frac{1}{2}$ cup sour cream

$\frac{1}{2}$ cup heavy cream

2 tablespoons chopped fresh flat-leaf parsley

$\frac{1}{2}$ teaspoon salt

$\frac{1}{4}$ teaspoon freshly ground black pepper

Preheat the oven to 350°F. Lightly butter an 8-inch square glass baking dish.

To make the breadcrumb topping: Heat the oil and butter in a small saucepan over medium-low heat. Add the garlic and cook (but do not brown), stirring occasionally, for 2 to 3 minutes. Add the breadcrumbs, stirring to toast evenly, and cook for 2 minutes. Remove from the heat and set aside.

To make the squash filling: Heat the oil and butter in a large skillet over medium-high heat. Add the onion, reduce the heat to medium-low, and cook, stirring occasionally, until very tender, 8 to 10 minutes. Add the squash and corn, raise the heat to medium-high, and cook, stirring often, until just tender, 3 to 4 minutes.

Remove from the heat; stir in the cheddar, sour cream, heavy cream, parsley, salt, and pepper; and mix well. Transfer to the prepared baking dish and sprinkle evenly with the breadcrumb topping. Bake, uncovered, for 30 to 40 minutes, until golden.

almond rice pilaf

makes 6 servings

When I want something just a little bit different or more interesting than plain rice for dinner, this fits the bill without much extra chopping or preparation.

2 tablespoons olive oil

1 tablespoon unsalted butter

1/2 cup finely chopped shallots

1 1/2 cups long-grain white rice

2 cups chicken stock

1 cup water

1 teaspoon salt

1/2 teaspoon garlic powder

1/2 teaspoon onion powder

1/2 cup chopped roasted almonds (see Note)

1/4 cup chopped fresh flat-leaf parsley

Heat the oil and butter in a large pot over medium-high heat. Add the shallots, reduce the heat to medium-low, and cook, stirring occasionally, until very tender, 8 to 10 minutes. Add the rice, and cook 2 to 3 minutes, stirring frequently, to lightly toast. Add the chicken stock, water, salt, and garlic and onion powders, stirring to combine all the ingredients. Raise the heat to high, cover, and bring to a boil.

Reduce the heat to very low, and simmer, covered, until all of the liquid has been absorbed by the rice, 15 to 20 minutes. Remove from the heat and stir in the almonds and parsley.

Note: To roast the almonds, place on a baking sheet in a 350°F oven for 15 minutes, or until lightly browned and fragrant.

macaroni and cheese

makes 8 to 10 side servings or
4 to 6 main-dish servings

I'm a huge macaroni and cheese fan, and I like to make it a bunch of different ways. This is my favorite "everyday, nothing fancy about it" macaroni and cheese recipe. The mixture of cheeses and touch of Tabasco give this casserole a little bite.

breadcrumb topping

2 teaspoons unsalted butter

½ cup plain breadcrumbs
(fresh if possible)

macaroni and cheese sauce

1 pound elbow macaroni

2 tablespoons unsalted butter

2 cups shredded Monterey Jack
cheese (6 ounces)

1½ cups shredded sharp white
cheddar cheese (4½ ounces)

1½ cups shredded Colby cheese
(4½ ounces)

½ cup (1 stick) unsalted butter

¼ cup all-purpose flour

2 cups whole milk

¼ cup sour cream (do not use
reduced-fat sour cream)

1 large egg

1 teaspoon Tabasco sauce

1 teaspoon Dijon mustard

1 teaspoon salt

Preheat the oven to 375°F.

To make the breadcrumb topping: Melt the 2 teaspoons of butter in a small saucepan over medium heat. Add the breadcrumbs and cook, stirring to toast evenly, for 2 minutes. Remove from the heat and set aside.

Put a large pot of water on to boil over high heat.

To make the macaroni and the cheese sauce: Cook the elbow macaroni according to the package directions, being careful not to over-cook. Drain the elbows. Return to the pot with the 2 tablespoons of butter and stir, off the heat, to coat evenly. Stir in 4 cups of the grated cheeses (reserving 1 cup). Set aside.

In a second large pot, melt the ½ cup of butter over medium-high heat until hot and bubbling. Add the flour, whisking constantly until well blended. Let the butter and flour cook, stirring occasionally, for 3 minutes. In a medium-size bowl, mix together the milk, sour cream, egg, Tabasco sauce, mustard, and salt. Gradually add the milk mixture to the flour and butter, whisking until thick and creamy, 3 to 4 minutes.

Add the cream sauce to the elbows, mixing thoroughly. Pour into a 3-quart casserole dish. Sprinkle with the remaining 1 cup of cheese and then the breadcrumbs. Bake uncovered for about 20 minutes or until golden and bubbly. Serve immediately.

cornbread apple-pecan dressing

makes 8 to 10 servings

I've been making this dressing with my Christmas turkey for as long as I can remember and it's also great, of course, with roast chicken or pork.

4 tablespoons (¹⁄₂ stick) unsalted butter

1 cup chopped yellow onion

³⁄₄ cup coarsely chopped celery

¹⁄₄ cup chopped fresh chives

1 tablespoon chopped fresh sage

1 tablespoon chopped fresh thyme

4 cups coarsely crumbled corn muffins (about 6 muffins, from your favorite recipe or a boxed muffin mix such as Jiffy), left out at least overnight, uncovered, to dry

2 cups cubed (¹⁄₂-inch cubes) white country or wheat sandwich bread, left out at least overnight, uncovered, to dry

2 cups chicken stock

1¹⁄₂ cups coarsely chopped peeled Granny Smith apples (about 2 medium)

1 cup coarsely chopped toasted pecans (see Note)

1¹⁄₂ teaspoons salt

¹⁄₂ teaspoon freshly ground black pepper

Preheat the oven to 375°F.

Melt the butter in a large skillet over medium heat. Add the onion and cook, stirring occasionally, for 5 minutes. Add the celery and continue cooking, stirring occasionally, for an additional 5 minutes.

Remove from the heat and stir in the chives, sage, and thyme. Transfer to a very large bowl, and allow to come to room temperature. Add the remaining ingredients and toss together until well combined (do not overmix). Transfer to a 2-quart casserole dish and bake uncovered for about 45 minutes, until golden brown on top.

Note: To toast the pecans, place on a baking sheet in a 350°F oven for 15 minutes, or until lightly browned and fragrant.

creamy mashed yukon gold potatoes

makes 6 servings

These are the perfect mashed potatoes. I like them with some lumps and I like to leave the skins on—I figure with all the cream and butter, I might as well get some vitamins from the potato skins to balance things out a bit.

3 pounds Yukon Gold potatoes, unpeeled, cut into ½-inch slices

1 cup half-and-half

½ cup (1 stick) unsalted butter, cut into pieces

1 teaspoon salt

Freshly ground black pepper

Put the potatoes in a large saucepan and cover with cold water by about 1 inch. Bring to a boil, cover the pot partially, and lower the heat to maintain a steady simmer. Cook until the potatoes are very tender when pierced with a fork, about 10 minutes. Drain the potatoes, return to the saucepan, and reduce the heat to low. Meanwhile, in a second saucepan, over very low heat, warm the half-and-half with the butter until the butter is melted. Using a hand masher, mash the potatoes until smooth. Stir in the half-and-half, butter, salt, and pepper to taste.

red potato, haricot vert, and cherry tomato salad

makes 4 servings

I like serving this instead of plain potato salad at summer barbecues—it's more interesting and certainly more colorful. The Dijon vinaigrette brings all the flavors together. This salad is also good with fingerling potatoes.

1 pound small red-skinned potatoes, unpeeled, cut into 1-inch pieces

1/3 pound haricots verts (thin French green beans), trimmed

1 cup halved cherry tomatoes

1/2 cup finely chopped red onion

5 tablespoons olive oil

2 tablespoons mayonnaise

1 tablespoon tarragon vinegar

1 tablespoon white wine

2 teaspoons Dijon mustard

1 teaspoon salt

1/4 teaspoon freshly ground black pepper

Put the potatoes in a large saucepan and cover with cold water by about 1 inch. Bring to a boil, cover the pot partially, and lower the heat to maintain a steady simmer. Cook until the potatoes are tender when pierced with a fork, about 10 minutes. Drain the potatoes in a colander, and allow to come to lukewarm temperature.

Bring a large saucepan of cold water to a boil. Add the beans and cook until crisp-tender, about 1 minute. Remove from the heat, drain, and rinse under cold water.

In a large bowl, combine the potatoes, beans, tomatoes, and red onion. In a separate small bowl, whisk together the remaining ingredients and toss with the potato mixture until well blended. This salad is best served at room temperature.

corn and cherry tomato salad with manchego cheese

This is a wonderful summer side dish. I like to serve it with grilled salmon or turkey burgers when I have friends over for a really casual meal. It's also an easy recipe to double or triple when asked to bring something to a barbecue because it travels really well.

3 cups fresh or frozen corn kernels

1 ½ cups halved cherry tomatoes

¾ cup finely chopped red onion

6 tablespoons olive oil

¼ cup chopped fresh flat-leaf parsley

3 tablespoons freshly squeezed lemon juice

Salt

Freshly ground black pepper

1 cup crumbled aged Manchego cheese (5 ounces) (see Note)

Bring a medium saucepan of cold water to a boil. Add the corn, cover, and cook until just tender, 2 to 3 minutes. Remove from the heat, drain, and place in a medium-size bowl with all of the ingredients except the cheese, and mix thoroughly. Serve at room temperature, with the Manchego cheese sprinkled on top.

Note: If you are unable to find the softer type of aged Manchego cheese that crumbles, you can substitute the more common type that has a cheddar-like consistency and grate it instead.

orzo with parmagiano and chives

Orzo is a nice alternative to rice or potatoes. This dish is especially good with baked or roasted chicken.

2 tablespoons unsalted butter

2 tablespoons olive oil

1/2 cup finely chopped yellow onion

1 tablespoon minced garlic

2 cups orzo

3 cups chicken stock

1 cup water

2/3 cup freshly grated Parmagiano-Reggiano cheese

1/2 cup finely chopped fresh chives

Salt

Freshly ground black pepper

Heat the butter and oil in a large saucepan over medium-high heat. Add the onion and garlic, reduce the heat to medium-low, and cook, stirring occasionally, until the onion is very tender, 8 to 10 minutes. Add the orzo, raise the heat to medium high, and cook, stirring often, until the orzo is lightly golden, about 3 minutes. Add the chicken stock and water, cover, and bring to a boil. Reduce the heat to very low and simmer until almost all of the liquid is absorbed, about 20 minutes. Remove from the heat and let stand, covered, for 5 minutes. Stir in the Parmagiano and chives. Season with salt and pepper to taste.

sweet potato casserole with almond-streusel topping

Every year we try out a new sweet potato dish for the Thanksgiving festivities. This is the latest and was a big hit with all. The recipe can easily be halved if you're not making it for the holidays.

streusel topping

1 cup all-purpose flour

2/3 cup firmly packed light brown sugar

6 tablespoons (3/4 stick) unsalted butter, softened and cut into small pieces

1 cup coarsely chopped pecans

casserole

6 pounds sweet potatoes

3/4 cup (1 1/2 sticks) unsalted butter, softened and cut into small pieces

One 8-ounce package cream cheese, softened and cut into small pieces

1/2 cup orange juice

1 teaspoon cinnamon

Preheat the oven to 425°F.

To make the streusel topping: In a medium-size bowl, mix together the flour and brown sugar. Using a pastry blender, cut in the butter until the mixture resembles coarse crumbs. (If you don't have a pastry blender, use a fork to cut the butter into the flour mixture.) Add the pecans and, using your hands, toss until all the ingredients are well combined. Set aside.

To make the casserole: Place the potatoes on a baking sheet lined with aluminum foil. Bake for about 1 hour, or until the potatoes can be easily pierced with a fork. Reduce the oven temperature to 350°F. Allow the potatoes to cool to lukewarm temperature.

When the potatoes are cool enough to handle, remove the skins. Place the potatoes in a large pot or bowl and mash until smooth. Add the butter, cream cheese, orange juice, and cinnamon and mix thoroughly. (It is much easier to blend in these ingredients when the potatoes are still warm.)

Transfer the mixture to a 3-quart casserole dish. Sprinkle evenly with the Streusel Topping. Bake for 25 to 35 minutes, or until the top is golden brown.

vegetables

string beans with roasted almonds and romano cheese

String beans are definitely my favorite vegetable, and this is probably my favorite way to prepare them. The combination of the almonds, the garlic, and the cheese is really wonderful. I like to use haricots verts for this recipe, but if you can't find them, use the thinnest green beans available.

1 pound string beans or haricots verts (thin French green beans)

1/2 cup coarsely chopped roasted almonds (see Note)

1/2 cup coarsely grated fresh Locatelli Romano cheese

4 tablespoons (1/2 stick) unsalted butter

3 tablespoons minced garlic

Bring a large saucepan of cold water to a boil. Add the beans and cook until crisp-tender, 1 to 2 minutes. Remove from the heat, drain, and rinse under cold water. Return to the saucepan with the remaining ingredients and cook over medium-high heat until the butter is melted and the ingredients are well blended, 3 to 4 minutes.

Note: To roast the almonds, place on a baking sheet in a 350°F oven for 15 minutes, or until lightly browned and fragrant.

sweet corn with scallions

makes 6 servings

Everyone seems to forget about corn when it's out of season, but there's really great tasting frozen corn available now all year round. This dish is so simple to prepare and so delicious. You can also use chives instead of the scallions if you happen to have them around.

4 1/2 cups fresh or frozen corn kernels

1/4 cup heavy cream

2 tablespoons unsalted butter

Salt

Freshly ground black pepper

1/2 cup chopped scallions (green parts only)

Bring a medium saucepan of cold water to a boil. Add the corn, cover, and cook until just tender, 2 to 3 minutes. Remove from the heat, drain, and return to the saucepan with the heavy cream and butter. Cook and stir over medium heat until the cream is slightly thickened, about 2 minutes. Season to taste with salt and pepper. Remove from the heat and stir in the scallions.

cauliflower gratin

Many of us overlook cauliflower when we're thinking about what to make for dinner. This vegetable dish looks very impressive but is incredibly easy to prepare.

1 pound cauliflower, cut into small florets (about 5 cups)

1 1/2 cups heavy cream

1/4 cup minced shallots

1/2 teaspoon salt

1/4 teaspoon white pepper

1 cup shredded Gruyere cheese (3 ounces)

Preheat the oven to 425°F.

Steam the cauliflower over boiling water until just tender, 3 to 4 minutes. Remove from the heat and set aside. Place the cream with the shallots in a large skillet. Bring to a boil over medium-high heat, uncovered, and continue to boil for 10 minutes.

Remove from the heat, and add the cauliflower, salt, and pepper. Transfer to a buttered 2-quart casserole dish. Sprinkle evenly with the Gruyere cheese. Bake, uncovered, for 10 minutes, until golden and bubbly.

garlic-dijon brussels sprouts

makes 6 servings

When I'm having people over for dinner, I try to make dishes that can be prepared in advance for the most part. Once the Brussels sprouts are cooked, they can be set aside, and then all you have to do is toss them with the rest of the ingredients until they're heated through.

1 1/2 pounds Brussels sprouts, trimmed

1/4 cup minced garlic

1/4 cup Dijon mustard

2 tablespoons unsalted butter

2 tablespoons olive oil

1/2 teaspoon salt

Bring a large saucepan of cold water to a boil. Add the Brussels sprouts, cover, and cook until tender, 8 to 10 minutes. Remove from the heat, drain, and return to the saucepan with the remaining ingredients. Cook over medium heat until the butter is melted and the ingredients are well blended, 3 to 5 minutes.

creamed spinach

makes 6 to 8 servings

This is a longtime favorite at our home. The cream cheese makes it extra creamy. And extra good. I know it seems like an awful lot of spinach, but keep in mind how much it cooks down.

½ cup (1 stick) unsalted butter

1 cup finely chopped yellow onion

3 tablespoons minced garlic

2½ pounds fresh baby spinach

One 8-ounce package cream cheese, cut into ½-inch cubes

2 tablespoons heavy cream

Salt

Freshly ground black pepper

Melt the butter in a large skillet over medium-high heat. Add the onion and garlic, reduce the heat to medium-low, and cook, stirring occasionally, until the onion is very tender, 8 to 10 minutes.

Add the spinach, about 5 ounces at a time, stirring with each addition, until the leaves are completely wilted. Add the cream cheese, stirring until melted and incorporated throughout. Stir in the heavy cream. Season to taste with salt and pepper.

green peas with onions

When you think you have no time to make a vegetable with your dinner, a simple recipe like this that complements just about any entree is the answer.

Two 10-ounce packages (about 4 1/2 cups) frozen green peas

3 tablespoons unsalted butter

1 cup finely chopped yellow onion

Salt

Freshly ground black pepper

Bring a medium saucepan of cold water to a boil. Add the peas and cook until just tender, 3 to 4 minutes. Remove from the heat, drain, and set aside. In the same saucepan, melt the butter over medium heat. Add the onion and cook, stirring occasionally, until very tender, 8 to 10 minutes. Stir in the peas. Season to taste with salt and pepper.

carrots with butter and parsley

makes 6 servings

The surprising ingredient in this recipe is the shallots, which give the carrots really great onion flavor without overpowering them. This dish is also great with broccoli and carrots mixed together.

1 1/2 pounds carrots, peeled and cut into 1/2-inch slices

3 tablespoons unsalted butter

1/2 cup finely chopped shallots

1/4 cup chopped fresh flat-leaf parsley

1/2 teaspoon salt

Bring a large saucepan of cold water to a boil. Add the carrots, cover, and cook until tender, about 10 minutes. Remove from the heat, drain, and set aside. In the same saucepan, melt the butter over medium heat. Add the shallots and cook, stirring occasionally, until tender, 5 to 7 minutes. Stir in the carrots, parsley, and salt.

desserts

peach crumbles

This is a perfect dessert for summer entertaining. It's really simple to put together since there's no crust to prepare, and yet it looks especially nice served in the individual dishes, especially when topped with some whipped cream.

topping

1 1/2 cups all-purpose flour

1 cup granulated sugar

1/2 cup firmly packed light brown sugar

3/4 cup (1 1/2 sticks) unsalted butter, softened and cut into small pieces

filling

4 cups blanched, sliced ripe peaches (6 to 8 medium) (see Note)

2 tablespoons granulated sugar

2 tablespoons cornstarch

Preheat the oven to 375°F.

To make the topping: In a large bowl, mix together the flour and sugars. Using a pastry blender, cut in the butter until the mixture resembles coarse crumbs. (If you don't have a pastry blender, use a fork to cut the butter into the flour mixture.) Set aside.

To make the filling: Place all the ingredients in a large bowl, and toss gently until the fruit is evenly coated. Spoon the fruit filling into eight 6-ounce glass custard dishes. Sprinkle the topping evenly over the fruit. Place the custard dishes on a baking sheet, and bake for 35 to 40 minutes, until golden. Serve warm, or at room temperature.

Note: To blanch the peaches, add them to a pot of boiling water, cook for 60 seconds, transfer to an ice water bath, and remove the skins before slicing.

brown sugar macadamia muffins

This sweet muffin is delicious eaten warm with butter and raspberry preserves.

2 cups all-purpose flour

1 cup firmly packed light brown sugar

2 teaspoons baking powder

$1/4$ teaspoon salt

1 cup whole milk

$1/2$ cup (1 stick) unsalted butter, melted and cooled slightly

2 large eggs, lightly beaten

1 teaspoon vanilla extract

$1 1/2$ cups coarsely chopped toasted macadamia nuts (see Note)

Preheat the oven to 400°F. Grease a 12-cup muffin tin, or line with paper liners.

In a large bowl, mix together the flour, sugar, baking powder, and salt, making sure that there are no lumps of brown sugar. Set aside.

In a medium-size bowl, beat together the milk, melted butter, eggs, and vanilla. Stir the liquid ingredients into the dry ingredients until just combined, being careful not to overmix. Gently stir in 1 cup of the macadamia nuts.

Spoon or scoop the batter into the muffin cups (they will be almost full). Sprinkle with the reserved ½ cup of nuts. Bake for 15 to 18 minutes, until lightly golden, or until a cake tester inserted into the center of the muffin comes out with moist crumbs attached. Serve warm.

Note: To toast the macadamias, place on a baking sheet in a 350°F oven for 12 minutes, or until lightly browned and fragrant.

cream cheese swirl brownies with heath bars and pecans

makes twenty-four 2-inch brownies

This is one of my favorite brownies because it's not too fudgy and it's not too cakey. Of course then you add the cream cheese, pecans, and Heath Bars and you have the perfect brownie . . .

cream cheese filling

One 8-ounce package cream cheese, not softened

1/3 cup sugar

1 large egg, at room temperature

2 tablespoons all-purpose flour

brownies

1 1/4 cups all-purpose flour

1 teaspoon baking powder

1/4 teaspoon salt

3/4 cup (1 1/2 sticks) unsalted butter

4 ounces unsweetened chocolate

2 cups sugar

3 large eggs, at room temperature

2 tablespoons whole milk

1 1/2 teaspoons vanilla extract

3/4 cup coarsely chopped toasted pecans (see Note)

2/3 cup chopped Heath Bars (about two 1.4-ounce bars) (or any chocolate-covered toffee bar)

Preheat the oven to 325°F. Grease and lightly flour a 13 x 9-inch baking pan.

To make the cream cheese filling: In a medium-size bowl, beat the cream cheese with the sugar until smooth. Add the egg and flour and beat well. Set aside.

To make the brownies: In a small bowl, combine the flour, baking powder, and salt. Set aside. In a medium-size saucepan over low heat, melt the butter with the chocolate, stirring occasionally, until smooth. Remove from the heat, transfer to a large bowl, and allow to cool to lukewarm, about 5 minutes. Stir in the sugar. Add the eggs, milk, and vanilla and beat well. Add the dry ingredients and mix thoroughly.

Stir in half of the pecans and half of the Heath Bars. Reserve 1/2 cup of the brownie batter. Spread the rest of the batter evenly in the prepared pan. Drop the cream cheese mixture by tablespoonfuls over the batter. Next, drop the reserved brownie batter by teaspoonfuls in between the cream cheese filling. Using a small knife, swirl the two batters together, forming a decorative pattern. Sprinkle the remaining pecans and Heath Bars over the top, and using a spatula, gently press into the batter. Bake for 45 to 55 minutes, or until a cake tester inserted in the center of the pan comes out with moist crumbs attached. Do not overbake. Allow to cool overnight before cutting and serving.

Note: To toast the pecans, place on a baking sheet in a 350°F oven for 15 minutes, or until lightly browned and fragrant.

strawberry icebox pie

There's nothing better in early summer than a dessert made with perfectly ripe in-season strawberries. This is one of my latest strawberry recipes—very simple, but very good.

crust

½ cup (1 stick) unsalted butter, melted

2 cups vanilla wafer crumbs

filling

5 cups fresh strawberries, sliced in halves

¾ cup sugar

¼ cup cornstarch

1 teaspoon vanilla extract

whipped cream topping

1 ½ cups heavy cream

1 ½ teaspoons sugar

1 ½ teaspoons vanilla extract

To make the crust: In a medium-size bowl, combine the butter and vanilla wafer crumbs. Press firmly into a lightly buttered 9-inch pie dish. Cover tightly with plastic wrap, and place in the freezer for 1 hour.

To make the filling: Mash 2 cups of the strawberries and place in a medium-size saucepan. Add the sugar and cornstarch, and stir constantly over medium heat, until the mixture is the consistency of fruit preserves, 10 to 15 minutes.

Reduce the heat to low, and continue cooking for 2 more minutes, until the mixture thickens slightly. Remove from the heat and stir in the vanilla. Transfer to a glass measuring cup and allow to cool to room temperature, about 15 minutes. Stir in the remaining berries and spread the filling evenly in the prepared crust. Cover with plastic wrap and chill the pie in the refrigerator for at least 4 hours and up to 8 hours.

To make the whipped cream topping: Place all the ingredients in a medium-size bowl and whip with an egg beater or a whisk, until soft peaks form.

Spread the whipped cream topping over the filling, or pipe decoratively, right before serving.

blackberry jam cake with white chocolate cream cheese frosting

makes one 2-layer 9-inch cake

This old-fashioned layer cake has blackberry jam mixed right into the batter. Traditionally it's iced with a very rich caramel frosting, but I like it with my favorite icing—white chocolate cream cheese—which balances out the sweetness of the cake really nicely.

cake

2²/₃ cups all-purpose flour

1 teaspoon baking soda

¹/₂ teaspoon salt

1 cup (2 sticks) unsalted butter, softened

1 cup granulated sugar

1 cup firmly packed light brown sugar

4 large eggs, at room temperature

1 cup buttermilk

1 teaspoon vanilla extract

1 cup seedless blackberry jam

1 cup chopped toasted pecans (see Note)

icing

Two 8-ounce packages cream cheese, softened

6 tablespoons (³/₄ stick) unsalted butter, softened

1 teaspoon vanilla extract

8 ounces white chocolate (such as Lindt—do not use a baking chocolate like Callebaut), melted and cooled to lukewarm temperature (see Note)

Preheat the oven to 350°F. Grease and lightly flour two 9 x 2-inch round cake pans, then line the bottom with a round of waxed paper.

To make the cake: In a small bowl, sift together the flour, baking soda, and salt. Set aside. In a large bowl, on the medium speed of an electric mixer, cream the butter until smooth. Add the sugars gradually, and beat until fluffy, about 3 minutes. Add the eggs, one at a time, beating well after each addition. Add the dry ingredients in three parts, alternating with the buttermilk and the vanilla. With each addition, beat until the ingredients are incorporated, but do not overbeat. Using a rubber spatula, scrape down the batter in the bowl, making sure the ingredients are well blended. Fold in the jam and pecans until no large pieces of jam remain, but leave some small bits throughout the batter. (Do not be alarmed when you see that the cake batter is actually purple in color—it will be brown when it comes out of the oven.)

Divide the batter between the prepared pans. Bake for 35 to 45 minutes, or until a cake tester inserted in the center of the cake comes out clean. Let the layers cool in the pan for 1 hour. Remove from the pan and cool completely on a wire rack.

To make the icing: In a large bowl, on the medium speed of an electric mixer, beat together the cream cheese and butter until smooth, about 3 minutes. Add the vanilla and beat well. Add the melted chocolate and beat well. Use immediately or store, covered, at room temperature for up to 4 hours.

½ cup chopped toasted pecans (see Note), for garnish

Fresh blackberries, for garnish (optional)

When the cake has cooled, spread the icing between the layers, stack the layers, then ice the top and sides of the cake. Garnish with pecans as desired. I also like to scatter a handful of fresh blackberries around the cake plate when they're in season.

Note: To melt the chocolate, place in a double boiler over simmering water over low heat, for approximately 5 to 10 minutes. Stir occasionally, until completely smooth and no pieces of chocolate remain. Remove from the heat and let cool for 5 to 15 minutes, or until lukewarm.

Note: To toast the pecans, place on a baking sheet in a 350°F oven for 15 minutes, or until lightly browned and fragrant.

sweet potato cheesecake with hazelnut crumb topping

makes one 10-inch
cheesecake

This is my newest Thanksgiving cheesecake creation. You can use yams instead of the sweet potatoes—they work equally well for this recipe. Be sure to start making the sweet potato purée for the cheesecake filling a few hours in advance (or you can make it a day in advance if you like and just bring to room temperature before proceeding with the recipe).

crust

1 cup cake flour (not self-rising)

1/4 cup firmly packed light brown sugar

1/2 cup (1 stick) unsalted butter, softened and cut into small pieces

3/4 cup chopped toasted hazelnuts (see Note)

crumb topping

3 tablespoons all-purpose flour

3 tablespoons granulated sugar

3 tablespoons firmly packed light brown sugar

6 tablespoons (3/4 stick) unsalted butter, softened and cut into small pieces

3/4 cup chopped hazelnuts

filling

Three 8-ounce packages cream cheese, softened

1/2 cup (1 stick) unsalted butter, softened

Preheat the oven to 350°F. Butter a 10-inch springform pan.

To make the crust: In a large bowl, mix together the flour and the sugar. Using a pastry blender, cut in the butter until the mixture resembles coarse crumbs. (If you don't have a pastry blender, use a fork to cut the butter into the flour mixture.) Add the hazelnuts and, using your hands, toss until all ingredients are well combined. Press into the bottom of the prepared springform pan.

Bake for 20 minutes. Remove from the oven and allow to cool on a wire rack. Lower the oven temperature to 325°F.

To make the crumb topping: In a medium-size bowl, mix together the flour and sugars. Using a pastry blender, cut in the butter until the mixture resembles coarse crumbs. (If you don't have a pastry blender, use a fork to cut the butter into the flour mixture.) Add the hazelnuts and, using your hands, toss until all ingredients are well combined. Set aside.

To make the filling: Place the cream cheese and butter in the bowl of a food processor fitted with a steel blade and process until very smooth. Add the sugars and mix well. Add the cooled sweet potato purée and process until the ingredients are well blended and no bits of sweet potato remain. Transfer the batter to a large bowl. Add the eggs, one at a time,

2/3 cup granulated sugar

1/3 cup firmly packed light brown sugar

1 cup sweet potato purée (about 3/4 pound) (see Note)

4 large eggs, at room temperature

3 tablespoons heavy cream

1 teaspoon vanilla extract

3/4 teaspoon cinnamon

stirring with a wooden spoon to combine. Stir in the heavy cream, vanilla, and cinnamon.

Pour the batter over the crust in the pan and set the pan on a baking sheet. Bake for 40 minutes. Slowly and carefully, remove the cheesecake (with the baking sheet) to add the topping. Sprinkle the crumbs evenly over the top of the cake and return it immediately to the oven. Bake for an additional 30 minutes.

At the end of the baking time, turn off the heat and, using a wooden spoon to keep the oven door slightly ajar, cool the cake in the oven for 1 hour. Remove the cake from the oven and allow it to sit at room temperature for another hour. Cover and refrigerate for at least 12 hours, or overnight. Remove the cake from the refrigerator 15 to 30 minutes before cutting and serving.

Note: To toast the hazelnuts, place on a baking sheet in a 350°F oven for 10 minutes, or until lightly browned and fragrant.

Note: To make the sweet potato purée: Place the sweet potatoes on a baking sheet and roast at 425°F for about 1 hour, or until a fork pierces through very easily. Allow to cool to room temperature (about 30 minutes), remove the skin, and mash with a potato masher.

apricot coconut squares

This bar cookie has a tender, flaky cream cheese crust with layers of apricot and coconut.

crust

1 cup all-purpose flour

½ cup (1 stick) unsalted butter, softened, cut into small pieces

3 ounces cream cheese, softened, cut into small pieces

topping

¾ cup sugar

1 large egg, at room temperature

1 teaspoon vanilla extract

1 cup sweetened shredded coconut

4 tablespoons (½ stick) unsalted butter, melted and cooled to room temperature

filling

⅓ cup apricot preserves

Preheat the oven to 375°F.

To make the crust: In a large bowl, on the medium speed of an electric mixer, beat together the flour, butter, and cream cheese until crumbly and well combined. Transfer the mixture to an ungreased 8 x 8-inch baking pan and, using your hands, pat the crust firmly and evenly into the pan. Bake for 20 minutes. Remove from the oven and allow to cool for 15 minutes.

To make the topping: In a medium-size bowl, on the medium-high speed of an electric mixer, beat together the sugar, egg, and vanilla until well combined. Stir in the coconut and the melted and cooled butter. Set aside.

Gently spread a thin layer of the apricot preserves filling over the prepared crust. Then, very carefully, spread the coconut topping over the entire top, being sure to go all the way to the edge. Bake for 18 minutes. Cool to room temperature, or overnight, before cutting and serving.

orange vanilla cupcakes

My friend Margaret Hathaway (who works with me on my cookbooks) came up with the idea for these cupcakes using the vanilla icing from the Red Velvet Cake at the bakery. She likes to tint the frosting pale pink. She'd also like me to mention that she thinks they're the perfect cupcake.

cupcakes

1 1/2 cups self-rising flour

1 1/4 cups all-purpose flour

1 cup (2 sticks) unsalted butter, softened

2 cups sugar

1 tablespoon freshly grated orange zest

4 large eggs, at room temperature

1 cup orange juice (use a variety without pulp)

1 teaspoon vanilla extract

frosting

3 tablespoons all-purpose flour

1 cup whole milk

1 cup (2 sticks) unsalted butter, softened

1 cup sugar

1 teaspoon vanilla extract

Sweetened shredded coconut, for garnish (optional)

Preheat the oven to 350°F. Line two 12-cup muffin tins with cupcake papers.

To make the cupcakes: In a small bowl, combine the flours. Set aside.

In a large bowl, on the medium speed of an electric mixer, cream the butter until smooth. Add the sugar and zest gradually and beat until fluffy, about 3 minutes. Add the eggs, one at a time, beating well after each addition. Add the dry ingredients in three parts, alternating with the orange juice and vanilla. With each addition, beat until the ingredients are incorporated but do not overbeat. Using a rubber spatula, scrape down the batter in the bowl to make sure the ingredients are well blended.

Carefully spoon the batter into the cupcake liners, filling them about three-quarters full. Bake for 20 to 25 minutes, or until a cake tester inserted into the center of the cupcake comes out clean. Cool the cupcakes in the tins for 15 minutes. Remove from the tins and cool completely on a wire rack before icing.

To make the frosting: In a medium-size saucepan, whisk the flour into the milk until smooth. Place over medium heat and cook, stirring constantly, until the mixture becomes very thick and begins to bubble, 8 to 10 minutes. Cover with waxed paper placed directly on the surface, and cool to room temperature, about 30 minutes.

In a large bowl, on the medium-high speed of an electric mixer, beat the butter for 3 minutes, until smooth and creamy. Gradually add the sugar, beating continuously, and mix until fluffy, for 3 minutes. Add the vanilla and beat well.

Add the cooled milk mixture, and beat for 5 minutes, until very smooth and noticeably whiter in color. Cover and refrigerate for 15 minutes (no less and no longer—set a timer!). Use immediately to frost the cupcakes. If you like, garnish with the coconut (or do some with coconut, and some without).

snickers icebox pie with chocolate wafer crust

makes one 9-inch pie

The idea for this very decadent dessert came one evening when I was dipping Oreos into a jar of peanut butter. (I hate to admit to these things in print, but yes, occasionally there is nothing like an Oreo cookie.)

crust

½ cup (1 stick) unsalted butter, melted

2 cups chocolate wafer crumbs

filling

One 8-ounce package cream cheese, softened

¾ cup confectioners' sugar

1 cup heavy cream

⅔ cup smooth peanut butter, at room temperature (do not use natural or old-fashioned style peanut butter)

1 ¼ cups chopped Snickers candy bars (about four 2.07-ounce bars)

To make the crust: In a medium-size bowl, combine the butter and chocolate wafer crumbs. Press firmly into a buttered 9-inch pie dish. Cover tightly with plastic wrap and place in the freezer for 1 hour.

To make the filling: In a large bowl, on the low speed of an electric mixer, beat the cream cheese until smooth, about 3 minutes. Add the sugar, and beat well.

In a separate bowl, beat the heavy cream until stiff peaks form. With a wooden spoon, stir the whipped cream into the cream cheese mixture, until no lumps of cream cheese remain. Cover and place in the refrigerator until ready to use.

Remove the crust from the freezer. Carefully spread the peanut butter in a thin layer over the bottom and half way up the sides of the crust. Sprinkle ¾ cup of the Snickers candy on top. Remove the cream cheese filling from the refrigerator and spread over the peanut butter layer. Sprinkle the remaining ½ cup of Snickers candy around the edge of the pie.

Cover tightly with plastic wrap and chill overnight in the refrigerator to set.

cinnamon pecan buns with cream cheese glaze

makes 8 buns

I've been working on this recipe for a while—a cinnamon bun made without yeast! These need to be eaten warm, pretty much straight out of the oven. That's usually no problem at my house. . . .

cinnamon pecan filling

½ cup (1 stick) unsalted butter, softened and cut into small pieces

½ cup firmly packed light brown sugar

1½ teaspoons cinnamon

¾ cup chopped toasted pecans (see Note)

cream cheese glaze

4 ounces cream cheese, softened and cut into small pieces

1 cup sifted confectioners' sugar

1 teaspoon whole milk

½ teaspoon vanilla extract

buns

2 cups all-purpose flour

1 tablespoon baking powder

1 teaspoon salt

¼ teaspoon baking soda

¼ cup canola oil

¾ cup buttermilk

Preheat the oven to 400°F. Lightly grease a 9 x 2-inch round cake pan.

To make the cinnamon pecan filling: In a medium-size bowl, on the medium speed of an electric mixer, beat together the butter, brown sugar, and cinnamon until smooth, 2 to 3 minutes. Stir in the pecans. Set aside.

To make the cream cheese glaze: In a small bowl, on the medium speed of an electric mixer, beat the cream cheese until smooth, 1 to 2 minutes. Add the sugar and beat well. Add the milk and vanilla and beat until smooth and creamy. Set aside.

To make the buns: In a large bowl, combine the flour, baking powder, salt, and baking soda. Add the oil and mix until well incorporated. Stir in the buttermilk until just blended. Gather the dough into a ball and knead on a lightly floured surface until smooth. Roll out the dough into a 15 x 8-inch rectangle.

Gently spread the cinnamon pecan filling evenly over the dough, leaving a ¼-inch edge all around. Roll up the dough into a tight cylinder, jelly-roll fashion, starting from one of the long sides. Press firmly to seal the edge, and turn the roll so that the seam is facing down. Using a serrated knife, cut the roll crosswise into eight 1½-inch-thick slices. Transfer the buns to the prepared pan, spacing them evenly. Bake 15 to 20 minutes, or until lightly golden. Remove from the oven and allow to cool for 3 to 4 minutes before drizzling very generously with the cream cheese glaze. Serve immediately.

Note: To toast the pecans, place on a baking sheet in a 350°F oven for 15 minutes, or until lightly browned and fragrant.

everyday chocolate cake

My favorite kind of chocolate cake—dark and rich and baked in a loaf pan—so it's really easy to cut slices when passing through the kitchen.

1 ½ cups all-purpose flour

¾ cup Dutch process cocoa

1 teaspoon baking soda

¼ teaspoon salt

½ cup (1 stick) unsalted butter, softened

1 cup firmly packed light brown sugar

½ cup granulated sugar

1 large egg, at room temperature

1 cup buttermilk

1 teaspoon vanilla extract

Preheat the oven to 325°F. Grease and lightly flour a 9 x 5 x 3-inch loaf pan.

In a small bowl, sift together the flour, cocoa, baking soda, and salt. Set aside.

In a large bowl, on the medium speed of an electric mixer, cream the butter until smooth. Add the sugars and beat until fluffy, about 3 minutes. Add the eggs and beat well. Add the dry ingredients in three parts, alternating with the buttermilk and vanilla. With each addition, beat until the ingredients are incorporated, but do not overbeat. Using a rubber spatula, scrape down the batter in the bowl, making sure the ingredients are well blended.

Pour the batter into the prepared pan. Place on a baking sheet and bake for 60 to 70 minutes, or until a cake tester inserted into the center of the loaf comes out clean. Allow to cool completely before serving.

banana pecan ice cream

This is the easiest ice cream in the world to make, and so incredibly rich, creamy, and delicious that no one will ever guess that you didn't slave over a custard base.

1 cup mashed very ripe bananas

One 14-ounce can sweetened condensed milk

¾ cup heavy cream

1 cup coarsely chopped toasted pecans (see Note)

In a medium-size bowl, stir together the bananas and milk. Add the cream and whisk until well blended. Pour the mixture into an 8 x 8 x 2-inch glass baking dish. Cover tightly with plastic wrap and place in the freezer for 2 hours, stirring every half hour. Pour into an ice cream machine and freeze until partially set, about 20 minutes. Stir in the pecans, and continue freezing until firm, about 5 more minutes, following the manufacturer's instructions.

Note: To toast the pecans, place on a baking sheet in a 350°F oven for 15 minutes, or until lightly browned and fragrant.

buttermilk cake with nectarines and vanilla cream

makes one 2-layer 9-inch cake

In the summertime, I love to make fruit desserts like this that aren't too rich or too heavy. Be sure to serve the cake soon after assembling it, otherwise the cream begins to melt!

cake

2 cups cake flour (not self-rising)

1 teaspoon baking powder

½ teaspoon baking soda

¼ teaspoon salt

½ cup (1 stick) unsalted butter, softened

1¾ cups sugar

1⅓ cups buttermilk

1 teaspoon vanilla extract

4 large egg whites, at room temperature (see Note)

vanilla cream

1½ cups heavy cream

2 tablespoons confectioners' sugar

2 teaspoons vanilla extract

nectarine filling

4 cups blanched, thinly sliced nectarines (about 6 to 8 medium) (see Note)

Preheat the oven to 350°F. Grease and lightly flour two 9 x 2-inch cake pans, then line the bottoms with waxed paper.

To make the cake: In a small bowl, sift together the flour, baking powder, baking soda, and salt. Set aside.

In a large bowl, on the medium speed of an electric mixer, cream the butter until smooth. Add the sugar gradually and beat until fluffy, about 3 minutes. Add the dry ingredients in three parts, alternating with the buttermilk and vanilla. With each addition, beat until the ingredients are incorporated, but do not overbeat. Using a rubber spatula, scrape down the batter in the bowl, making sure the ingredients are well blended and the batter is smooth.

In a separate small bowl, beat the egg whites on the high speed of an electric mixer until soft peaks form. Gently fold into the batter. Divide the batter between the prepared pans and bake for 20 to 25 minutes, or until a cake tester inserted into the center of the cake comes out clean.

Let the cakes cool in the pans for 1 hour. Remove from the pans and cool completely on a wire rack.

To make the vanilla cream: In a large bowl, whip the heavy cream with the sugar and vanilla until stiff peaks form.

To assemble the cake: When the cake layers have cooled completely, spread half of the vanilla whipped cream over the bottom cake layer, followed by half of the nectarines. Place the second cake layer on top of the

nectarines and top with the remaining cream and nectarines. Serve immediately.

Note: It is best to separate the eggs when cold and then allow them to come to room temperature before proceeding with the recipe.

Note: To blanch the nectarines, add them to a pot of boiling water, cook for 60 seconds, transfer to an ice water bath, and remove the skins before slicing.

granola cookies with white chocolate and roasted almonds

makes 4 dozen cookies

I like to use Quaker 100% natural cereal (the Oats & Honey variety—without the raisins) to make these cookies. It's a little sweeter than most granolas and has a touch of coconut in it.

2 cups all-purpose flour

1 teaspoon baking soda

1/2 teaspoon salt

1 cup (2 sticks) unsalted butter, softened

1/2 cup granulated sugar

1/2 cup firmly packed light brown sugar

1 large egg, at room temperature

1 teaspoon vanilla extract

1 1/2 cups granola

1 cup coarsely chopped roasted almonds (see Note)

2/3 cup coarsely chopped white chocolate (such as Lindt)

In a small bowl, combine the flour, baking soda, and salt. Set aside.

In a large bowl, cream the butter with the sugars until smooth, about 2 minutes. Add the egg and vanilla, and beat well. Add the dry ingredients and mix thoroughly. Stir in the granola, almonds, and white chocolate.

Drop by rounded teaspoonfuls onto ungreased cookie sheets, leaving several inches between for expansion. Place the cookie sheets in the refrigerator and chill for 20 minutes. Meanwhile, preheat the oven to 350°F.

Bake the cookies for 12 to 14 minutes. Cool the cookies on the sheets for 5 minutes, then remove to a wire rack to cool completely.

Note: To roast the almonds, place on a baking sheet in a 350°F oven for 15 minutes, or until lightly browned and fragrant.

apple cream cheese crumb pie

makes one 9-inch pie

I came up with this recipe for my dad. It combines two of his favorite desserts—cheesecake and apple crumb pie. Although there are three layers in the pie, don't worry; it's neither difficult nor time-consuming to prepare.

crumb topping

1 ½ cups all-purpose flour

1 cup packed light brown sugar

⅔ cup (1 ⅓ sticks) unsalted butter, softened and cut into small pieces

cream cheese filling

One 8-ounce package cream cheese (not softened)

⅓ cup sugar

1 large egg, at room temperature

1 teaspoon vanilla extract

¼ teaspoon salt

apple filling

3 tablespoons sugar

1 tablespoon all-purpose flour

⅛ teaspoon cinnamon

⅛ teaspoon salt

3 cups peeled, cored, and sliced tart apples, such as Winesap or Granny Smith (about 4 medium)

crust

1 cup plus 2 tablespoons all-purpose flour

Preheat the oven to 425°F.

To make the crumb topping: In a medium-size bowl, mix together the flour and sugar. Using a pastry blender, cut in the butter until the mixture resembles coarse crumbs. (If you don't have a pastry blender, use a fork to cut the butter into the flour mixture.) Using your hands, toss until all the ingredients are well combined. Set aside.

To make the cream cheese filling: In a medium-size bowl, on the medium speed of an electric mixer, beat together the cream cheese and sugar until smooth and creamy. Add the egg, vanilla, and salt, continuing to beat until the ingredients are well blended and the mixture is considerably thicker, 3 to 5 minutes. (I recommend using the whisk attachment if your mixer has one.) Set aside.

To make the apple filling: Place the sugar, flour, cinnamon, and salt in a large bowl. Add the apples and toss gently until the fruit is evenly coated. Cover tightly with plastic wrap and set aside.

To make the crust: Place the flour in a large bowl and, using a pastry blender, cut in the shortening until the pieces are pea-size. (If you don't have a pastry blender, my editor, Justin, suggests that you can also use two knives, in a crossing pattern, to cut the shortening into the flour mixture.) Sprinkle the ice water by tablespoonfuls over the flour mixture and toss with a fork until all of the dough is moistened. Gather the dough into a ball and roll it out on a lightly floured surface to fit a 9-inch glass pie dish and

½ cup solid vegetable shortening

3 tablespoons ice water

trim, leaving ½ inch around the edge. Fold the edges under all around the rim, and crimp.

Spread the cream cheese filling evenly in the bottom of the crust. Gently spread the apple filling over the cream cheese. Sprinkle the crumb topping evenly over the fruit. Place the pie on a baking sheet.

Lower the oven temperature to 350°F and bake for 65 to 75 minutes, or until the apples are tender and the crumb topping is golden brown. This pie is best served at room temperature, not warm.

chocolate cupcakes with butterscotch frosting

**These cupcakes are very rich and very chocolatey and the butterscotch
frosting is the perfect complement.**

cupcakes

2 cups cake flour (not self-rising)

1 teaspoon baking powder

½ teaspoon salt

½ cup (1 stick) unsalted butter,
softened

1 cup firmly packed light brown sugar

½ cup granulated sugar

2 large eggs, at room temperature

6 ounces unsweetened chocolate,
melted (see Note)

1⅓ cups whole milk

1 teaspoon vanilla extract

frosting

½ cup (1 stick) unsalted butter

⅔ cup firmly packed dark brown
sugar

½ cup heavy cream

3 cups confectioners' sugar

1 teaspoon vanilla extract

Preheat the oven to 350°F. Line two 12-cup muffin tins with 18 cupcake
papers.

To make the cupcakes: In a small bowl, sift together the flour, baking
powder, and salt. Set aside.

In a large bowl, on the medium speed of an electric mixer, cream the butter until smooth. Add the sugars and beat until fluffy, about 3 minutes. Add
the eggs, one at a time, beating well after each addition. Add the chocolate,
mixing until well incorporated. Add the dry ingredients in three parts,
alternating with the milk and vanilla. With each addition, beat until the
ingredients are incorporated but do not overbeat. Using a rubber spatula,
scrape down the batter in the bowl, making sure the ingredients are well
blended, and the batter is smooth. Carefully spoon the batter into the cupcake liners, filling them about three-quarters full. Bake for 20 to 25 minutes,
or until a cake tester inserted into the center of the cupcake comes out
clean.

Cool the cupcakes in the tins for 15 minutes. Remove from the tins and cool
completely on a wire rack before frosting.

To make the frosting: Melt the butter in a medium-size saucepan
over medium-low heat. Add the brown sugar and whisk constantly for
5 minutes. Gradually add the cream, and continue whisking for 2 more
minutes. Remove from the heat, transfer to a large bowl, and allow to cool
to room temperature, 10 to 15 minutes, stirring occasionally.

On the medium speed of an electric mixer, gradually add the confection-ers' sugar, beating continuously until smooth. Add the vanilla and beat well. Continue to beat, on the medium speed, for an additional 5 minutes until very creamy, noticeably lighter in color, and of thicker consistency. Use immediately to frost the cupcakes or store, covered, at room temperature for up to 4 hours.

Note: To melt the chocolate, place in a double boiler over simmering water on low heat for approximately 5 to 10 minutes. Stir occasionally until completely smooth and no pieces of chocolate remain. Remove from the heat and let cool for 5 to 15 minutes, or until lukewarm.

pineapple cheesecake with white chocolate sauce and macadamias

makes one 10-inch
cheesecake

The idea for this was inspired by a dessert I had at one of our favorite hotels, Roundhill Resort in Jamaica. They served a pineapple cheesecake there with white chocolate ice cream on top, and the flavors were so great together, I came home from vacation and started baking! This just might be my all-time favorite cheesecake recipe.

crust

½ cup (1 stick) unsalted butter, melted

1¼ cups graham cracker crumbs

¾ cup chopped toasted macadamia nuts (see Note)

¼ cup sugar

filling

Four 8-ounce packages cream cheese, softened

1¼ cups sugar

5 large eggs, at room temperature

2 cups crushed canned pineapple, drained thoroughly!

2 tablespoons heavy cream

1 tablespoon vanilla extract

white chocolate sauce

12 ounces white chocolate, such as Lindt, coarsely chopped

½ cup heavy cream

1 cup coarsely chopped toasted macadamia nuts, for garnish (see Note)

Preheat the oven to 350°F.

To make the crust: In a medium-size bowl, combine the butter, graham cracker crumbs, macadamia nuts, and sugar. Press into the bottom of a buttered 10-inch springform pan. Bake for 10 minutes. Remove from the oven, and allow to cool on a wire rack. Reduce the oven temperature to 325°F.

To make the filling: In a large bowl, on the low speed of an electric hand mixer, beat the cream cheese until very smooth. Gradually add the sugar. Add the eggs one at a time. To ensure that the batter has no lumps and that no ingredients are stuck to the bottom of the bowl, stop the mixer several times and scrape down the sides of the bowl with a rubber spatula. Stir in the pineapple, heavy cream, and vanilla.

Pour the filling over the crust and set the pan on a baking sheet. Bake until the edges are set and the center moves only slightly when the pan is shaken, about 1 hour. At the end of the baking time, turn off the heat, and using a wooden spoon to keep the oven door slightly ajar, cool the cake in the oven for 1 hour. Remove the cake from the oven and allow to sit at room temperature for another hour. Cover and refrigerate for at least 12 hours, or overnight. Remove the cake from the refrigerator 15 to 30 minutes before cutting and serving.

To make the white chocolate sauce: In a small saucepan, over very low heat, combine the white chocolate with the heavy cream. Stir until the white chocolate is completely melted and the sauce is smooth, 3 to 5 minutes. Remove from the heat and transfer the sauce to a glass measuring cup. Allow to cool to room temperature, about 30 minutes. Remove the cheesecake from the pan and pour the sauce over the entire top of the cheesecake (letting it drip down the sides) and garnish with the macadamia nuts.

Note: To toast the macadamias, place on a baking sheet in a 350°F oven for 12 minutes, or until lightly browned and fragrant.

christmas vanilla sugar cookies

makes about 3 dozen cookies

I love this Christmas cookie recipe because the dough is very easy to handle and roll out, and the cookies look really pretty and festive with the cream colored icing and white sugar without having to do any fancy decorating. I like to use a snowflake-shaped cookie cutter, but a regular round cutter is fine too.

cookies

2 1/2 cups all-purpose flour

1 teaspoon baking powder

1/4 teaspoon salt

1 cup (2 sticks) unsalted butter, softened

1 cup sugar

2 large egg yolks, at room temperature

2 teaspoons vanilla extract

icing

1/2 cup plus 2 tablespoons confectioners' sugar

1/4 cup heavy cream

1/4 teaspoon vanilla extract

White decorating sugar, for garnish

To make the cookies: In a small bowl, sift together the flour, baking powder, and salt. Set aside. In a large bowl, cream the butter and sugar until smooth, about 2 minutes. Add the egg yolks and vanilla and beat well. Add the dry ingredients, in three parts, and mix until just combined. Shape the dough into three flat disks, wrap each disk tightly with plastic wrap, and refrigerate for 30 minutes. Working with one disk at a time, roll out the dough on a lightly floured surface to 1/4-inch thickness. Using a 2½-inch fluted cutter, cut out the cookies and place on baking sheets lined with waxed paper. Place the baking sheets in the refrigerator and chill for an additional 15 minutes. Meanwhile, preheat the oven to 375°F and grease two baking sheets.

Remove the cookies from the refrigerator and arrange on the greased baking sheets, 2 inches apart. Bake for 9 to 11 minutes, until lightly golden around the edges. Cool the cookies on the sheets for 5 minutes, then remove to a wire rack to cool completely.

To make the icing: In the top of a double boiler, over simmering water, combine all of the ingredients. Stir for 2 to 3 minutes until smooth. Remove from the heat, transfer to a glass measuring cup, and allow to cool to lukewarm before using.

To ice the cookies: Using a pastry brush, spread a light coating of icing on each cookie and then sprinkle the decorating sugar over the icing. (Let the icing set for a few hours before stacking the cookies.)

blueberry coffeecake with cinnamon crumbs

makes one 10-inch cake or
about 18 buns (see Note)

This is a really moist coffeecake with lots of blueberries and a hint of cinnamon in the crumb topping—the perfect not-too-sweet breakfast treat.

crumb topping

1 ½ cups all-purpose flour

1 cup granulated sugar

½ cup firmly packed light brown sugar

½ teaspoon cinnamon

¾ cup (1 ½ sticks) unsalted butter, softened and cut into small pieces

cake

1 ¾ cups all-purpose flour

1 teaspoon baking powder

½ teaspoon baking soda

½ teaspoon salt

One 8-ounce package cream cheese, softened

½ cup (1 stick) unsalted butter, softened

1 cup granulated sugar

2 large eggs, at room temperature

¼ cup whole milk

1 teaspoon vanilla extract

1 ½ cups fresh blueberries, lightly coated with flour

Preheat the oven to 325°F. Grease and lightly flour a 10-inch tube pan, or about 18 bun cups or large muffin cups.

To make the crumb topping: In a medium-size bowl, mix together the flour, the sugars, and the cinnamon. Using a pastry blender, cut in the butter until the mixture resembles coarse crumbs. (If you don't have a pastry blender, use a fork to cut the butter into the flour mixture.) Set aside.

To make the cake: In a small bowl, sift together the flour, baking powder, baking soda, and salt. Set aside.

In a large bowl, on the medium speed of an electric mixer, beat together the cream cheese, butter, and sugar until smooth, 2 to 3 minutes. Add the eggs and beat well. Add the dry ingredients in two parts, alternating with the milk and vanilla. Fold in the blueberries.

Pour the batter into the prepared pan (or bun cups) and sprinkle evenly with the crumb topping. Bake for 50 to 60 minutes for the tube cake (or 20 to 25 minutes for the buns), or until a cake tester inserted into the center of the cake comes out clean. Let the cake cool in the pan for 1 hour. Remove from the pan and cool completely on a wire rack.

Note: Bun pans are available at Bakerscatalogue.com (or 1.800.827.6836). They offer a hamburger bun pan (item #5185) or a large square muffin pan (item #5362)—my new favorite for making buns.

caramel almond toffee crunch ice cream

One of the things that drives me crazy about store-bought ice cream is when you have to dig around the container with your spoon searching for the Heath Bars. When you make your own ice cream you can put in as many Heath Bars as you like (and almonds) (and caramel swirls).

caramel

½ cup sugar

¼ cup half-and-half

2 tablespoons unsalted butter

1 tablespoon light corn syrup

ice cream

6 large egg yolks, at room temperature

⅔ cup sugar

2 cups half-and-half

1 cup heavy cream

1 tablespoon vanilla extract

¾ cup coarsely chopped roasted almonds (see Note)

½ cup coarsely chopped Heath Bars (about 1½ 1.4-ounce bars)

To make the caramel: In a medium-size saucepan, heat the sugar over medium heat, stirring, until it melts and turns a light amber color. Stir in the half-and-half, butter, and corn syrup, and continue stirring until smooth and thick, about 2 minutes. Remove from the heat and allow to cool to room temperature. Wrap tightly with plastic wrap and refrigerate until completely chilled, preferably overnight.

To make the ice cream: In a medium-size bowl, with an eggbeater or a whisk, beat the egg yolks until creamy, 2 to 3 minutes. Add the sugar and beat until incorporated. Set aside. In a double boiler, over simmering water, scald the half-and-half. Add ½ cup of the half-and-half to the egg mixture, stirring to warm the egg yolks. Return the entire mixture to the double boiler and continue to cook, stirring constantly, until the mixture coats the back of the spoon, about 10 minutes. Remove from the heat and place the pot in a bowl of cold water. Cool the custard to room temperature (about 45 minutes), stirring once about halfway through to prevent a skin from forming on the top. When the custard has cooled to room tempera-ture, stir in the heavy cream and vanilla. Cover and refrigerate until completely chilled, preferably overnight. Pour into an ice cream machine and freeze until partially set, about 20 minutes. Stir in the almonds and Heath Bars, and continue freezing until firm, about 5 more minutes, follow-ing the manufacturer's instructions. Turn off the ice cream machine, and using a small offset spatula or knife, swirl in the caramel.

Note: To roast the almonds, place on a baking sheet in a 350°F oven for 15 min-utes, or until lightly browned and fragrant.

sour cream peach streusel buns

makes 12 buns (see Note)

I like to make breakfast buns all year long, and when peaches are in season, these are really wonderful.

streusel topping

1 cup all-purpose flour

1 cup sugar

1/2 teaspoon cinnamon

1/2 cup (1 stick) unsalted butter, softened and cut into small pieces

buns

1 1/2 cups cake flour (not self-rising)

1 teaspoon baking powder

1/2 teaspoon baking soda

1/4 teaspoon salt

6 tablespoons (3/4 stick) unsalted butter, softened

3/4 cup sugar

1 large egg, at room temperature

1 large egg yolk, at room temperature

1 teaspoon vanilla extract

3/4 cup sour cream (do not use reduced-fat sour cream)

1 1/2 cups blanched, peeled, and coarsely chopped ripe peaches (about 2 to 3 medium) (see Note)

Preheat the oven to 350°F. Grease and lightly flour 12 bun cups or large muffin cups.

To make the streusel topping: In a medium-size bowl, combine the flour, sugar, and cinnamon. Using a pastry blender, cut in the butter until the mixture resembles coarse crumbs. (If you don't have a pastry blender, use a fork to blend the butter into the flour mixture.) Set aside.

To make the buns: In a small bowl, sift together the flour, baking powder, baking soda, and salt. Set aside. In a large bowl, on the medium speed of an electric mixer, cream the butter until smooth. Add the sugar gradually and beat until fluffy, about 3 minutes. Add the egg, egg yolk, and vanilla and beat well. Add the dry ingredients and mix until just combined. Stir in the sour cream. Fold in the peaches.

Spoon the batter into the bun cups. Sprinkle the topping over the buns, being sure to keep the crumbs within the muffin cups (otherwise the buns are difficult to remove from the pan). Bake for 20 to 25 minutes, or until a cake tester inserted into the center of the bun comes out clean.

Note: To blanch the peaches, bring a large pot of water to a boil, add the peaches, and blanch for 1 minute. Transfer to an ice water bath to cool and remove the skins before chopping.

Note: Bun pans are available at Bakerscatalogue.com (or 1.800.827.6836). They offer a hamburger bun pan (item #5185) or a large square muffin pan (item #5362)—my new favorite for making buns.

hazelnut buttermilk pie

makes one 9-inch pie

A simple, old-fashioned, not-too-sweet custard pie with a crunchy hazelnut topping. You might not think to serve whipped cream with a custard pie, but I like whipped cream on all pies.

crust

1 cup plus 2 tablespoons all-purpose flour

½ cup solid vegetable shortening

3 tablespoons ice water

filling

3 large eggs, at room temperature

1 large egg yolk, at room temperature

1 cup granulated sugar

¼ cup firmly packed light brown sugar

¼ cup all-purpose flour

1 teaspoon vanilla extract

½ teaspoon salt

6 tablespoons (¾ stick) unsalted butter, melted and cooled to room temperature

¾ cup buttermilk

1¼ cups chopped hazelnuts

Preheat the oven to 400°F.

To make the crust: Place the flour in a large bowl and, using a pastry blender, cut in the shortening until the pieces are pea-size. (If you don't have a pastry blender, my editor Justin suggests that you can also use two knives, in a crossing pattern, to cut the shortening into the flour mixture.) Sprinkle the ice water by tablespoons over the flour mixture, and toss with a fork until all the dough is moistened. Gather the dough into a ball, roll out on a lightly floured surface to fit a 9-inch glass pie dish, and trim, leaving ½ inch around the edge. Fold the edges under all around the rim and crimp. Prick all over the bottom and sides of the crust with a fork. Place the crust on a baking sheet and bake for 12 minutes. Remove from the oven and allow to cool to room temperature, about 35 minutes.

Lower the oven temperature to 350°F.

To make the filling: In a large bowl, beat together the eggs, egg yolk, and sugars, until creamy and well blended, about 2 minutes. Add the flour, vanilla, and salt and beat well. Add the melted butter and beat well. Stir in the buttermilk.

Pour the filling into the cooled crust. Sprinkle the hazelnuts evenly over the top of the pie.

Return to the oven and bake for 45 to 50 minutes, or until the center of the pie is set. Cool on a wire rack for at least 4 hours before cutting and serving. This pie is best served at room temperature, not warm.

apricot cream cheese tart with gingersnap pecan crust

This past summer the apricots at the market were so delicious, I was inspired to make this dessert. There's a reason that icebox desserts became popular in the summertime when there's no need to turn the oven on. Even the crust for this tart goes into the freezer, instead of being baked.

crust

1/2 cup (1 stick) unsalted butter, melted

1 1/2 cups gingersnap cookie crumbs

1/2 cup chopped toasted pecans (see Note)

filling

Two 8-ounce packages cream cheese, softened

1 cup confectioners' sugar

1/4 cup sour cream (do not use reduced-fat sour cream)

1 teaspoon vanilla extract

topping

2 1/2 cups thinly sliced fresh ripe apricots (5–8 apricots—apricots vary widely in size depending on the variety)

3 tablespoons apricot preserves

To make the crust: In a medium-size bowl, combine the butter with the gingersnap crumbs and pecans. Press firmly into a buttered 10-inch tart pan with removable bottom. Cover tightly with plastic wrap and place in the freezer for 1 hour.

To make the filling: In a large bowl, on the low speed of an electric mixer, beat together the cream cheese and sugar until smooth and creamy. Add the sour cream and vanilla, continuing to beat at low speed until well combined.

Remove the tart pan from the freezer and spread the filling evenly in the crust with a rubber spatula. Arrange the sliced apricots on top of the filling in a decorative manner. In a small saucepan over low heat, warm the apricot preserves, stirring often, for 1 to 2 minutes. Remove from the heat, and lightly brush the apricots with the warmed preserves. Refrigerate the tart for at least 4 hours, or overnight, to ensure that the filling sets.

Note: To toast the pecans, place on a baking sheet in a 350°F oven for 15 minutes, or until lightly browned and fragrant.

peanut butter blondies with white chocolate and pecans

I love blondies, and I love to come up with new and interesting blondie recipes. This one has all of my favorite flavors in one bar cookie—it's sweet and rich and really fantastic.

1 cup all-purpose flour

1/2 teaspoon baking powder

1/4 teaspoon baking soda

1/4 teaspoon salt

1/2 cup (1 stick) unsalted butter, softened

1/2 cup smooth peanut butter, at room temperature (do not use natural or old-fashioned style peanut butter)

3/4 cup firmly packed light brown sugar

1/4 cup granulated sugar

1 large egg, at room temperature

2 teaspoons vanilla extract

3/4 cup coarsely chopped toasted pecans (see Note)

1/2 cup peanut butter chips

1/2 cup coarsely chopped white chocolate (preferably Lindt)

Preheat the oven to 325°F. Grease and lightly flour an 8-inch square baking pan.

In a small bowl, combine the flour, baking powder, baking soda, and salt. Set aside.

In a large bowl, cream the butter with the peanut butter and the sugars until smooth, 2 to 3 minutes. Add the egg and vanilla and beat well. Add the dry ingredients and mix thoroughly. Stir in the pecans, peanut butter chips, and the white chocolate, reserving 2 tablespoons of each.

Spread the batter evenly in the prepared pan. Sprinkle the reserved pecans, chips, and white chocolate evenly over the top and, using a spatula, gently press into the batter. Bake for 30 to 35 minutes, or until a cake tester inserted in the center of the pan comes out with moist crumbs attached. Do not overbake. Allow to cool to room temperature or overnight before cutting and serving.

Note: To toast the pecans, place on a baking sheet in a 350°F oven for 15 minutes, or until lightly browned and fragrant.

index

notes

notes